POLLSTERS TELL US when they survey 10 Roman Catholics, eight of them classify themselves as gamblers. That makes Catholics unchallenged leaders in an ecclesiastical hierarchy of gaming enthusiasts. Not far behind, however, are the Jews. Gambling participation among synagogue members is pegged at 77 percent. Presbyterians and Episcopalians are neck-and-neck at 74 percent, with a comfortable lead over the 63 percent of Methodists who admit to gambling tendencies.

Only 43 percent of Baptists surveyed say they gamble, while 33 percent of the members of nondenomination-al groups, including the traditionally conservative Bible Churches, admit they do a little betting now and then. That figure sounds low when compared to the denominations, but it means that one out of every three conservative Christians may have no scruples against gambling!

T.W., Jr.

DON'T BET ON IT

TOM WATSON JR.

Regal Books

A Division of GL Publications
Ventura, California, U.S.A.

Published by Regal Books
A Division of GL Publications
Ventura, California 93006
Printed in U.S.A.

Library of Congress Catalog in Publication Data

Watson, Tom, 1918-
    Don't bet on it.

    1. Gambling—Religious aspects—Christianity.
2. Gambling—United States.   I. Title.
HV6713.W37   1987   363.4'2'0973   86-31575
ISBN 0-8307-1013-2

1 2 3 4 5 6 7 8 9 10 / 91 90 89 88 87

Rights for publishing this book in other languages are contracted by Gospel Literature International (GLINT) foundation. GLINT also provides technical help for the adaptation, translation, and publishing of Bible study resources and books in scores of languages worldwide. For further information, contact GLINT, Post Office Box 488, Rosemead, California, 91770, U.S.A., or the publisher.

Contents

9

An Inside Look at Casinos

"Money when it enters the casino no longer signifies confidence, security, promise or well-being, and it certainly has no connection with the work or will of God."

119

10

Loopholes and High Rollers

"Gambling casinos provide enticing tax advantages for those wily enough to claim them and a no-questions-asked laundering facility for 'dirty' money."

139

11

Managing the Point Spread

"Enterprising bookies can net $10,000 in clear profit in a good week with properly managed point spreads, and it is doubtful that they tithe that income to support the work of the Lord."

153

12

The Elusive Alfie Mart

"Alfie lives by an ethical system uniquely his own. 'The gambler's business is the most honorable of all,' he insists."

167

13

Enforcement of Gambling Laws

"We Christians must lead in a new assessment concerning the benign or malignant qualities of gambling operations and the appropriate punishment, if any, for law violations."

181

14

Gambling as a Sickness

"Curiously, little has been said or done by evangelical Christians to address the problem of compulsive gambling."

197

15

The Gamblers Anonymous Solution

"The Gamblers Anonymous program addresses a dream world common to all compulsive gamblers—a world unfathomable to the nongambler because it lies in territory uncharted by the rational mind."

221

16

The Case in a Nutshell

"There are well-meaning if undiscerning Christians who consider gambling a harmless recreational diversion and see no moral or spiritual reason to deny themselves or others that pleasure."

235

Acknowledgment

The danger is grave
that credit for a book,
should it merit credit at all,
will be given to the author alone
because his name appears on the cover.
In the case of *Don't Bet on It!*
that would be a very serious
miscarriage of justice.

This page is an effort, therefore,
to set the record straight.
Without the insights,
the patience
and the professional skills
of its editor, it would never have
made it as far as the printing press.

It is published with gratitude to
Earl Roe
Managing Editor
Regal Books

Introduction: What's All the Fuss?

Three-fourths of all Americans queried in a variety of polls now "see nothing wrong with gambling." If you share that sentiment as a Christian, you are the victim of a massive confidence game that is draining the moral, spiritual and—yes, even the financial resources of our nation.

No, this is not a book about some satanic Communist plot to enslave us to the Russians, but it *is* about a devilish and deliberate conspiracy. It is a cry of alarm, and it is intended for the ears of those naively willing to sacrifice their own integrity and the well-being of their children—plus generations yet to come—on the altar of gambling's empty promises.

A Notorious Human Weakness

This book is an exposé of a plot that exploits human weakness in a felonious transfer of wealth from the pockets of those who cannot afford the loss to the pockets of those who purpose to have it all.

The field is fertile. During the course of any given year, two-thirds of all Americans wager money—legally or otherwise—on some sort of chance outcome. Most of them lose, but that doesn't stop them from betting. The money that changes hands each year in illegal betting alone now surpasses the preposterous total of our national deficit. The ranks of sick, tormented, compulsive gamblers in our society are expanding at a rate that terrifies psychologists and social workers whose job is to pick up the pieces. If the trend continues, human devastation through the sinister addiction of gambling will surpass even the agony spawned by chronic drunkenness.

It has not always been that way in America. Gambling has been regarded since time immemorial as a notorious defect of character, but public disapproval and the united testimony of Christians until now has limited its disruptive influence on our society. The laws against it at times were flouted and mocked, but they served to hold it in check.

Today, in contrast, gambling fever is sweeping our nation. Too few seem to care; too many actually celebrate. Indeed, it is increasingly difficult to find even believers in Christ who are sure of their own convictions when the question of legalized gambling arises. Fanned by this ambivalence, the flames of decriminalized gambling continue to spread across our nation like some loathsome disease of the soul. Shockingly, that disease is welcomed far more often than it is shunned in too many segments of our society.

Some on that irrational welcoming committee are Christians, and that is the most disturbing fact of all. The widespread acceptance of gambling—especially as a source of public revenue—threatens to erase yet another line of clear distinction between citizens of the Celestial City and those whose dwelling place is called Destruction. Too many have forgotten that neither the righteousness of God nor His will for His people is subject to the whims of public sentiment or the shifting sands of majority opinion.

I Write Because I Am Outraged

I have written this book because I am both a Christian and an American, and under both of those classifications I am outraged. I am an evangelical; a former Presbyterian pastor and foreign missionary. I am an author, a marriage counselor and a business consultant. I am a conservative but not an obscurantist. I have tried my hand at gambling and listened respectfully and attentively to its proponents. I have interviewed also many of its victims. I have participated in two successful Florida campaigns under two governors to defeat proposed constitutional amendments to legalize casinos on a countywide basis. As a Christian and as an American, I must share my discoveries with others who care.

When a woman pushes a cart heavily loaded with gourmet foods past a California checkout counter and pays for her groceries with food stamps, a meritorious welfare program is only mildly abused. When at the same counter she lays down a $20 bill for lottery tickets, an entire value system goes down the drain. An isolated incident? Perhaps. Yet a Christian who was next in line and who had voted for the lottery says the experience prompted a dramatic change—lamentably too late—in his point of view.

But is there a difference between a book on the evils of gambling and a book on the sinfulness of smoking, dancing, movies or the other shibboleths that fundamentalists opposed so vehemently a couple of decades ago? Have we not outgrown the legalism that prompted schism and distrust wherever the faithful laid down arbitrary rules and regulations for acceptable Christian behavior?

Yes, I believe we have outgrown the legalism, and I intend to show you there is, indeed, a difference. What we will be talking about in the chapters that follow is not rules and regulations but greed, corruption, personal tragedy and the prostituting of an important principle of faith.

I will show you the debilitating and often irreversible effects of the compromise known as gambling on the society we share and on the faith that binds us to God.

1
A Clear View of a Murky Issue

THE ISSUE MAY BE MURKY for some, but one thing is as clear as the waters caressing the casino-lined beaches of the Bahamas: In anybody's language, laying money on the line in hopes of instant wealth has become big, big business in America. Unless a rational force of resistance is mounted, this business is going to get bigger still.

Winning—or more often, losing—on the turn of a roulette wheel, the roll of the dice, the flip of a card, the pull of a slot machine handle, the fall of a number or the score of an athletic contest now enjoys a broadening legitimacy and public acceptance undreamed of only a couple of decades ago. Each year, either by referendum, by legislation or by personal compromise, more Americans enthusiastically embrace legalized—often state-controlled—gambling as a versatile cure-all against both personal boredom and the mounting cost of government.

But what are we doing to the Body of Christ when Christians, too, participate? As His "kingdom of priests"

(Rev. 1:6, *Phillips*), do we trust in our High Priest or in a heathen concept of luck? Under the terms of the Ten Commandments, we are denied the indulgence of coveting and stealing. We are to acquire another man's wealth only in exchange for goods or services—or as a voluntary gift. We testify to the world that our Saviour supplies everything we really need "according to his riches in glory" (Phil. 4:19). By what perverted rationalization do we undermine that faith by seeking our wealth from the fickle hands of some goddess of chance?

Here and there, a stubborn old warrior of the faith might speak out against this newest step toward moral and spiritual oblivion, but few, if any, heed the warning. People who consider themselves enlightened seem to prefer the oblivion. Advocates of legalized gambling ridicule as narrow and shortsighted any objection to a permissive society where vices are legitimized and human weakness is exploited in the name of fun, games and government funding.

Who Speaks Against Compromise?

For people in whom Jesus Christ dwells and over whose lives He rules and reigns, what is our appropriate posture on an issue that speaks so eloquently of covetousness, greed and avarice? In fact—quite apart from Christian commitment—what should the response be of multiplied thousands of unchurched men and women of good will who long to breathe freely the air of a clean, honest, sane and crime-free society? Surely no mystical level of spiritual insight is required to recognize the systematic self-destruction that already has our soci-

16

ety floundering on the shoals of vice and corruption. Lawmakers across the nation are capitulating—often in spite of their own better judgment—to the public clamor for lotteries, casinos and other forms of legalized gambling. Have Christians lost the will to speak out against such compromise?

While the rest of the nation celebrates, where are those who dare cry alarm? Along with the whoremonger, the "covetous man, who is an idolater," (Eph. 5:5) has no inheritance in the kingdom of Christ. "Because of these things cometh the wrath of God upon the children of disobedience. Be not ye therefore partakers with them" (vv. 6,7). The Word of God contains no specific "Thou shalt not gamble," but it speaks with painful clarity on the subject of thievery, greed and extortion.

Our Nobleness of Spirit

If there is any validity at all in the idea that a nation's greatness relates in part to strength of character and nobleness of spirit among its people, then our fascination with government revenue from gambling must be viewed with a sense of impending doom. The funding of our government from sources that prey upon weaknesses—that exploit the frailties of human nature—is not calculated to strengthen the fiber of our nation. Neither will it draw us closer to God.

The fact is, government-sponsored gambling is more likely to encourage defiance of the law and a spirit of revolution among those already inclined to view our system with hostility and cynicism. The lottery, for example, can be seen as a bizarre new form of discrimination. The same people whom the law denies any right

17

to organize and profit from gambling for themselves—because somehow it is a threat to our mutual well-being—are asked to become its willing victims so that the state may prosper. That irrationality is not the foundation upon which our nation was built. In a democratic republic, the state exists for the people, not the people for the state.

A functioning "government of the people, by the people and for the people" bound together as "one nation, under God" assumes certain ethical prerequisites—chief among them being the ideal of common good. Even some state lawmakers who reluctantly support the legitimizing of gambling fear those ethical prerequisites are dangerously lacking in the way state lotteries are operated.

Chief among these ethical requirements is a sense of mutual responsibility on the part of the people who are governed. Without that sense of shared involvement—expressed both in personal concern and in public allegiance—we would not deserve the freedom and dignity inherent in a healthy democracy. What is more, we would not be likely to get it or to keep it very long.

The Social Costs of Gambling

Writing in USA TODAY, psychologist Julian I. Taber warns that "No one knows the social costs of gambling or how many players will become addicted because the states, ignoring the concerns of experts on compulsive gambling, have failed to do any research before leaping into the gambling business. The states are experimenting with the minds of the people on a massive scale."[1]

Taber fears the unemployed, the uneducated, the

moderately retarded, the isolated old, the widowed with empty lives and the very young all will be made "the new victims of state greed." His research has shown that most lottery customers suffer to some degree a common delusion, identified through psychological research done with clinical groups of compulsive wagerers. They see gambling as something more than mere recreation; it appears as a way for players to solve their problems. All too often, the result of that erroneous perception is a disastrous worsening of the problems they sought to resolve.

That is why our sense of personal pride and civic responsibility is eroded as more and more government is financed with proceeds from gambling schemes. The prospect of national strength and individual loyalty is considerably more favorable when money for the function of government is derived from equitably assessed and duly collected tax revenue—from each according to his ability to pay.

"Fair" May Be Elusive

Admittedly, the word, "equitable," raises inevitable problems where taxes are concerned. In our imperfect world, "fair" and "equitable" become relative terms wherever they are applied—but that cynical truth need not eliminate the concept of equity in sharing the cost of government. Fairness may be elusive in any frame of reference, but occasional inequities in the assessment and collection of taxes—even the apparently inevitable inconsistencies—need not warrant the abandonment of taxation as the proven and preferred basis for government funding.

Whatever the legitimized gaming enterprises, they imply the transfer of the burden of supporting government from a tax base to a percentage of the take from games of chance. That transfer will deprive citizens of their sense of personal involvement in the means by which government is financed. More than that, a subtle inequity emerges. Those who do not gamble get a free ride—with all of the benefits and none of the responsibilities.

Points to Ponder

1. Some forms of gambling now enjoy increasing acceptance and legitimacy, even though gambling generally was regarded as a criminal activity during most of this century. People's ideas, value systems and mores do change over the years, but under what circumstances might morals—"right" and "wrong"—change?

2. Lawmakers historically have considered gambling a threat to the general welfare and, in their wisdom, have classified it, along with others, as a vice. Was that a mistake that needed correcting?

3. If the Bible does not speak specifically on the subject of gambling, what principles should we examine that might shed some light on the attitude God takes toward this widespread human indulgence? Is covetousness—or perhaps even stealing—really a factor in a person's gambling habit?

4. Do you think the funding of government through lot-

teries instead of through a system of taxation might be a threat, however subtle, to the nobleness of spirit and unity of purpose that made America great?

5. As government gets more and more involved in gambling enterprises, what responsibility do you feel it has toward those who are victimized because their gambling habit is out of control?

Note
1. Julian I. Taber, in "Opinion," USA TODAY, [August 14, 1984], p. 4.

2
Taking the Easy Way Out

PROPONENTS OF LEGALIZED state lotteries and casinos as a means of raising government revenue are so preoccupied with the forest that the ghostly shape of the trees escapes them. In the main they are pragmatists, but as such they seem intent upon sacrificing the enduring upon the altar of the immediate.

To the pragmatists, revenue from gambling is an unobjectionable, uncomplicated, tested, workable and effortless way to fill the gaps in government budgets. "People are going to gamble anyway, whether it is legal or not," they reason. They remind us that participation in the games is voluntary. To them legalized and taxed gambling offers a safe political haven in the tempest constantly buffeting those who struggle to bring government budgets into balance.

Next: a Government-Sponsored National Lottery

Are you aware that a strong movement already is underway to lead America's voracious federal government into the weed-choked pastures of lottery revenue? With that goal established, who knows what the next target will be in the movement toward the legitimizing of vices?

To the unthinking citizen whose attention is riveted only on holding the line on taxes while increasing government handouts, powerful forces in this country make what seems a convincing case for taking the wraps off all forms of gambling—and some would include other vices as well—and de-criminalizing them in order to channel proceeds to the public benefit instead of to illegal operators. If you tend to shrug off that decriminalization as unlikely, consider the fact that in nearly half of our 50 states, citizens have been offered, through the democratic process, the opportunity to test their luck in government-sponsored lotteries. They have seized upon that new permissiveness with great relish. People from all walks of life—and, yes, from a variety of church relationships—dutifully and enthusiastically participate by religiously purchasing their lottery tickets—aware though some may be of the horrendous odds against them.

Lotteries: "Something for Everyone"

The pragmatists can present convincing evidence to confirm the success of lotteries. The total take from state-sponsored games rose from $5.3 billion in 1983 to $6.7 billion in 1984 and $8 billion in 1985. Few, if any, find cause for complaint when dazzled by these figures. State treasuries are gleaning a combined total of nearly $2.5 billion each year from lotteries. Almost as much as that is handed out each year to prizewinners, and certainly none of these instant millionaires would find fault with the system.[1]

Pennsylvania has created more than 100 millionaires since the inauguration of its lottery, and other hopeful participants easily picture themselves the next to enter those worry-free ranks. Odds calculators splash a little cold water on that dream however. Some reckon that a person is *3.5 times more likely to be killed by lightning* and *five times more likely to be eaten by a shark* than he is to win a state lottery jackpot!

All state lotteries offer fat commissions for ticket sellers, and that fact enlists the support of supermarket and convenience store operators and other vendors who welcome a new source of revenue. Their percentage usually is 5 percent of their gross sales. Other administrative costs soak up more than $600 million from the total intake each year.

One persistent argument in favor of state lotteries is that they do offer legislators an apparent solution for their perplexing fiscal dilemma. Lotto is a handy way to raise revenue without raising taxes, and Americans are growing more and more resistant to new taxes. Harry A. Johnston II, 1985-86 President of the Florida Senate, predicted that "lotteries will be with us during the next three years." His reasoning is typically pragmatic and disturbingly lacking in statesmanship: "Rather than increase taxes *we will take the easy way out* (italics mine) and go to the lottery," he writes.[2]

A Fickle Source of Income

But lotteries prove a fickle source of income for states that elect to go that route. When California began

25

its lottery in October 1985, it grossed $8.4 million during the first week. By the second week of January 1986, the gross had fallen to less than half that much. Sales in California bottomed out at slightly more than $3 million two months later, prompting Lottery Director Mark Michalko to innovate in May a "Second Chance" gimmick that selects 50 $2,500 winners out of all the losing tickets. The strategy pulled the California lottery out of its summer doldrums.[3]

In 1981, the Arizona lottery's opening week generated an unanticipated $5.4 million. Enthusiasm ran high among legislators and administrators, and proponents of state lotteries everywhere rubbed their hands with glee. A year later, however, the gross had dropped 83 percent to only $900,000 a week. Lottery officials then recognized the importance of innovation and excitement, and of vigorous marketing of their product.

"In lottery operations," says Douglas Gordon, executive director of the District of Columbia's lottery, "you have to keep innovating to be successful."[4] That means you must market your product. State lotteries flounder when they do nothing more than passively serve the needs of citizens in search of opportunities to gamble. Lottery managers must create that desire.

A passive service is not enough to meet their financial goals. They must fan the flame. They must make converts from the ranks of nongamblers, and—like yet undiscovered alcoholics—one in 20 of these will be gripped by a new and unsuspected compulsion once that first wager is made.

Lottery states must motivate experienced gamblers to gamble more. They must make Lotto exciting—the "in thing." And while doing all that they must compete with other gambling enterprises—legal and illegal alike—most of which offer significantly better odds.

Proponents Say It Is "Voluntary"

"It's strictly voluntary," the proponents of state-sponsored gambling insist—meaning, presumably, that no one influences anyone else to flush his money down the state lottery drain. In the proponents' rationale, that "voluntary" aspect appears to remove all ethical restraints.

Consider the alcoholic, however, if you are open to a new perspective on the word. His drinking surely is voluntary, quite aggressively so. No one feeds him alcohol intravenously, or forces down his throat the booze that destroys him. He drinks it by his own volition. The drug addict, too, snorts, swallows, inhales or injects his fix of his own free will. The victim of obesity opens the refrigerator door voluntarily to stuff another snack in his mouth or down another beer.

Most of us have found that the human will under pressure is a weak and unreliable ally. Our will seldom functions ethically as a truly free agent. Most of us have discovered, often to our embarrassment or shame, that our will is subject to a wide variety of powerful human compulsions, and these are not always attuned to the perfect will of God.

"It was completely voluntary when I bet my family's grocery money on an ill-fated filly at Aqueduct," an admitted compulsive gambler in New Jersey retorted when asked to comment on state funding through the "voluntary" taxes derived from lotteries. The distorted sense of values that enslaved his will drove him to physi-

27

cal, financial, emotional and marital ruin before he was able to acknowledge his sickness. He is among the few who seek help to bring them back from the brink of personal disaster.

Christians should find themselves concerned about the potential dangers of a source of government revenue dependent upon human greed and weakness of will. Informed believers should have second thoughts about their government's role in fanning the flame of that against-all-odds hope of instant wealth that impoverishes more often than it enriches. The purchase of lottery tickets is far from voluntary when sponsoring states budget millions each year for media blitzes to lure new players into the act.

For followers of Jesus Christ, gambling is an insidious form of worldliness. If our citizenship truly is in heaven (see Phil. 3:20) and our supply comes from God (see 4:19), then we cannot harmonize that faith with the testing of fate called "gambling." The kind of greed—and fantasy—that goes hand-in-hand with wagering can motivate people to squander on lottery tickets and other forms of gambling assets better spent on the necessities of life for themselves and for their families, on helping the unfortunate or on the evangelizing of a lost world. When the state hustles them to hand over that money in the futile hope of instant riches, they are not taxpayers; they are victims. In the vocabulary of the gamblers, they are "pigeons." They are not blessed; they are duped. They are not served; they are exploited.

A Regressive Form of Taxation

Moreover, state lotteries as funding devices—unlike

28

traditional tax formulas—tend to produce income for the state in reverse proportion to the earning levels, and thus the tax liability, of its citizens. As an alternative to tax revenue, lotteries are regressive and, therefore, unfair.

Figures released by the Illinois Legislative Council support that conclusion. Residents of prosperous suburban DuPage County, west of Chicago, out-earn other Illinois citizens with their $14,000 per-capita income, but they provide per-capita lottery revenue of only $15—next to the lowest in the state. In contrast, Cook County, composed primarily of Chicago with its $7,000 income per person, accounts for a surprising $46.26 in per-capita lottery revenue.

"Lottery revenue" in Illinois refers to the state's take of only 41 percent of the money actually wagered. The amount of money wagered is more than twice what the revenue is. That means the average DuPage County resident—wealthier than his counterpart in other areas of the state—purchases $36 worth of lottery tickets each year, while the average Cook County resident, with considerably less "discretionary" income—and perhaps equally inadequate discretion?—wagers about $112, more than three times as much as his wealthier west-suburban neighbors.

Let us reduce that to an even more basic concept. Earnings from the Illinois lottery are that state's alternative—in part—to revenue from taxes. Resorting to that alternative prompts people who earn half as much money as their more affluent neighbors to pump three times as much money into the state's coffers. That is what we mean by "regressive" taxation.

Poor people outnumber rich people wherever we go, and the lotteries show us that less affluent citizens are the ones more likely to take a chance on making that big win of a lifetime. They are more willing to risk what little they have against the possibility of lasting freedom from the disheartening economic uncertainties that threaten to plague them at the end.

"As bad as things are," they reason, "they won't be much worse, if I risk a few bucks each week on winning the jackpot. But I'll be a heck of a lot better off if I'm the lucky one, and the more I bet the better my chances of winning." Those "chances of winning," in a sense, become the object of their faith. Sadly, in the case of 99.99999 percent of these misled citizens, that line of reasoning and that object of faith result in a steady, debilitating drain on their already inadequate finances. That, too, is what we mean by "regressive."

A Step Toward Legalized Casinos

But compulsive behavior and regressive taxation are not our only objections to state-sponsored lotteries. Such lotteries are deliberately designed, in addition to their other purposes, to strengthen the case for legalized casinos in the several areas where initiatives are pending. When Hollywood, Florida public relations professional Jay Kashuk was gathering signatures on petitions urging a state lottery in Florida, he told the *Miami Herald* on March 19, 1982, that the lottery scheme was designed as "a public relations tool to ease the feelings toward the word, 'casino.'" With that statement he gave substance to what other proponents had dismissed as merely a "paranoid fear."

Kashuk is one of the organizers of the persistent Committee for Florida State Lotteries, and is identified with Castaways Hotel owner Charles Rosen, Fontainbleu Hotel owner Stephen Muss and Marco Polo Hotel owner Bennett Lifter in an untiring initiative to legalize casinos on Miami Beach. Kashuk's statement confirms the fact that a state lottery would be perceived by some as the first step toward overcoming the stubborn resistance disenchanted Floridians mount against casino gambling.

The Ethical Conflict

These facts make Christians part of a complicated ethical conflict. Some state lawmakers themselves confess to experiencing dilemma as they ponder the relative merits of easing the tax burden through revenue from gambling.

"In New Jersey," writes Assistant Minority Leader Chuck Hardwick, assemblyman from his state's twenty-first district, "the public debated ethics when they considered the lottery and later the casinos. By their affirmative vote, in our democratic society, they have decided the ethical questions on whether there should be gambling, so now, the new ethical issues center around how gambling is to be conducted, and the state's responsibility to those who are hurt by it."[5]

Here are the political and ethical questions with which the New Jersey Legislature now struggles:

- To what extent should gambling be promoted to induce people to start gambling, or to gamble more?

- What promotional messages are appropriate?

31

- What role, if any should credit have in gambling? How easy should it be to get credit? Should credit limits be compared to income?

- What should be the rules concerning casino conduct for hours of operation, free liquor while gambling, and other enticements for people to enter casinos?

Hardwick believes states contemplating taking the plunge into gambling should delve deeply into all the facts before making a decision. "I would urge any state considering expansion of any form of gambling to study New Jersey and other high gambling states to profit from our mistakes," he says. He has specific suggestions for those intent upon following his state's example:

There should be a dedication of revenues from the very beginning to confront identifiable social problems, such as compulsive gambling, which may not be evident until gambling has been in place in a state for a while.

I doubt that the proponents of the gambling industry are greedier than other businesses [There are those who take a less charitable view!], but their privileged position places them in a strong advantage over many vulnerable members of the public. Consequently, the laws concerning the industry's activities should be stringent so the public isn't relying

32

upon the industry's discretion or good will.[6]

These are haunting ethical considerations. They require carefully authenticated answers before even our secular society launches prematurely its determined gambling revenue programs.

When a Nation's Character Is at Stake

In the early 1800s, poet William Blake included this terse observation in a characteristically blunt social statement he hoped would provide guidance for his fellow Englishmen. Nearly two centuries later, Blake's little rhyme (circa 1815) still has a certain subtle relevancy:

> The whore and gambler, by the state
> Licensed, build that nation's fate.[7]

When the character or the future of a nation is at stake, it behooves its citizens to weigh carefully the broader issues involved, however strong their personal passions may be, and to consider all the consequences before making a decision of such magnitude. Factors other than raw dollar figures must be dealt with. The disturbing questions demanding answers begin with this: Are a few more dollars in the state treasury a satisfactory trade-off for the aggressive encouragement of a notorious human weakness, the undermining of the work ethic, the compromise of our faith and the lowering of personal values that such a reckless strategy will encourage? Is the revenue anticipated from legalized gambling really worth the fantasy it stimulates and the human misery and instability it generates? Is there not a logical basis for the fear that the "big bucks" available to gambling entrepeneurs offer an open invitation to even more fraud and corruption in our already troubled land?

It is true that public sentiment in the past has swung to the permissive at historical watersheds, only to return in due time to a more cautious and conservative view. Usually it was men of Christian commitment who influenced that occasional cooling of human passions. Left to its own resources, that pendulum likely will continue its tireless arc, arriving every century or so at opposite extremes on the scale of moral and ethical perception. Yet at this particular moment in history, gambling, particularly as a means of government funding, is the new obsession of what is assumed to be a rational and responsible citizenry.

Perhaps we can do no more than speculate—dare we say, "gamble on it"?—as to the consequences of that obsession until we have run once again the full cycle that saw gambling prohibited in this country—for whatever reasons—a century or more ago.

Reducing the Cost of Government

The compelling notion itself, however, that more money must be channeled into government coffers by whatever method it takes to achieve it raises a separate issue of enormous significance. Yes, we are to "render unto Caesar what is Caesar's" (see Mark 12:17), but is there not a limit on what Caesar can justly and reasonably demand of his citizens? That is a question deserving careful and courageous reflection as the gambling issue is pondered. Is the escape from our cost-of-government dilemma a simple matter of finding always more revenue, no matter how much our standards or our spiritual well-being are compromised in the process? Or is it more realistic and more productive to bury the gambling issue once and for all—without mourning—and address with determination the question of how to reduce government spending?

A frightening proportion of that spending most certainly has its roots in poor judgment, boondoggling, ineptness, unconscionable waste, special interest lobbying and out-and-out corruption. Must Christians—to whom all government is of God—cynically accept these abuses as inevitable and be made accessories by this specious reasoning? Is the only available solution the desperate funneling of more money into government, even if we must victimize our fellow citizens by siphoning it from the wallets of gambling pigeons?

I think not!

Points to Ponder

1. Pragmatically, lotteries do produce large sums of money for their sponsoring states—large sums, that is, until you compare the take with the total state budget. Lottery revenue averages only 2 or 3 percent of the revenue from tax and fee sources. If gambling really isn't in the best interest of the American people, does that relatively small amount of state income justify ignoring our responsibility and "gambling" on the possible harm lotteries might inflict upon our people?

35

2. Do you feel "taking the easy way out" is an acceptable expression of the responsibility that must be shouldered by those who make, interpret or enforce our laws?
3. What is the possible flaw in the reasoning that betting on the numbers to be drawn in a state lottery is *voluntary* and, therefore, poses no risk or potential danger to the public?
4. Why do you think people who can least afford to lose apparently are most likely to place bets in state lotteries? Can the state's efforts to persuade people to buy Lotto tickets be construed as a breach of faith by misleading them into an unrealistic expectation of winning?
5. To what degree do you feel the financial squeeze of government—reflected in budget deficits—can be laid at the feet of excessive government spending rather than on the government's inability to raise enough money?

Notes
1. *State Legislatures,* March 1986.
2. Harry A. Johnston, II, letter to the author, January 17, 1985. Used by permission.
3. *Miami Herald,* May 15, 1986.
4. *Public Gaming,* March 1985, p. 32.
5. Chuck Hardwick, letter to the author, May 31, 1984. Used by permission.
6. Ibid.
7. William Blake, "Auguries of Innocence," *The Oxford Dictionary of Quotations* (London: Oxford University Press, 1966), p. 74.

3
Promises, Promises!

Our PROBLEM WITH THE COST of government—most particularly with the juggling of deficits—grows out of a tragically false and illogical concept of what government is supposed to be. And that same concept is yet another mark of our national and—all too often—personal biblical illiteracy. Our present national economic crisis springs in part from the wild, irresponsible and ruinous spending habits that have come to characterize our government at virtually every level.

Corruption, greed, collusion, lack of scruples, misguided philanthropy, a naive, unscriptural and do-good concept of social responsibility—plus, now and then, sheer stupidity—combine all too often to make our government a shockingly inefficient and ruinously costly indulgence. One of the remarkable aspects of our democracy is the fact that our spendthrift concept of government is grudgingly tolerated by the relatively intelligent but demonstrably masochistic citizens who bear without complaint the burden of its costs.

If it has not yet become one of those "laws"—like

Murphy's or Demetrius's—then perhaps it is time we recognize this truth as such: *no matter how trivial or how impromptu the cause for finding additional "temporary" government revenue, once the addition to the budget has been made the secularists who largely control the political apparatus inevitably will declare it a fixed and essential expense.*

Demand an Alternative to "More Money"

For this and other reasons, Christians simply are not obliged to accept at face value the proposition that our government must forever find new sources of revenue in order to function effectively. That increasingly frantic search for revenue leads inevitably to a lowering of public scruples as to how we get it. There always are alternatives other than "more money," but too few will shoulder the responsibility of finding them. Ever seeking new sources of public revenue serves only to exacerbate the reckless spending problem and create the need for yet more money to pay the bills.

The ruling faction in the American political system can always dream up novel ways to spend newly discovered revenue—either on themselves, on their political allies, on their social theories or on whatever it takes to perpetuate themselves as officeholders. Under the protective mantle of "separation of church and state," they are careful to see that it is not spent on advancing the Kingdom of God.

"But," the proponent of legalized casinos and state lotteries is inclined to argue, "when we talk about legalizing gambling we are talking about reducing the cost of government. We're talking about huge sums of money pouring into state coffers—tax money from casinos and the state's 'take' from lotteries. The whole point here is to get money for things like education, roads and our elderly without the necessity of new taxes. With this new source of revenue we will certainly reduce the tax load."

New Ways to Spend Are Only a
Few Steps Behind

But pledges that lotteries and casinos—or whatever form of gambling we legitimize—will reduce the citizen's tax load are specious at best. At worst, they are deliberate deceptions. Again and again they have proved broken promises. The fact is, they have yet to reduce the actual cost of government to the private citizen wherever they have been tried. After more than half a century of casino revenue, Nevada still finds it necessary to levy a 5 percent sales tax on all retail purchases. It has no better schools, no better roads, no more generous senior citizen benefits than most other states. The citizens of lottery states find they pay as much in taxes as they ever did; their state just spends more. In government, those who think up new ways to spend government revenue are only a few steps behind those who engineer new ways to rake it in.

Gambling—the motivation of greed notwithstanding—has indeed demonstrated its ability as a source of significant revenue to help meet that relentless demand for more government services. That ability would have merit, however, only if meeting that demand were our chief legitimate concern. It is not; our concern is to redefine the role of government and lower the cost. We need a serious legislative crusade to lift the tax burden. Rather than lower costs, revenue from legalized gambling enterprises serves all too often to escalate extravagance in government spending.

The apparent motivation for some who favor legalized casinos or a state-sponsored lottery is the reasoning that all this new revenue for the state will come from the pockets of *someone else,* from a source as yet untapped. Therefore, it will save the rest of us money. Though they may be an endangered species, a few rational citizens do act logically on their awareness that insuperable odds rob them of any logical expectation of emerging substantial long-term winners. Those whose decisions are governed by that rationality are not likely to indulge in the wagering game. If they favor legalized gambling, therefore, it is because they see it as a discriminatory tax on their less rational fellow citizens who do indulge—and that makes them glad.

"Love . . . does not pursue selfish advantage," Paul wrote in his classical definition of *agape.* "It does not keep account of evil or gloat over the wickedness of other people. On the contrary, it shares the joy of those who live by the truth" (1 Cor. 13:5,6, *Phillips*).

A Tax on Those Who Risk Their Financial Stability

Some thoughtful Americans are beginning to contend that we are taxed already at federal, state, county and municipal levels far beyond what can be considered reasonable, fair or even necessary. Each year taxes take a larger and greedier slice of the pie. Support for state lotteries and other legalized and taxed gambling schemes aims at adding yet another digit or two to the cost of government. The fact that the cost is placed on the shoulders—or wallets—of those greedy enough and irrational enough to buck the odds does not make right the inequity. Government revenue from gambling is a tax imposed upon those willing to trade their own financial stability for a spark of hope that someday, against all odds and counter to any logical expectation, they will stumble onto the mythical pot of gold at the foot of the rainbow.

Conscientious Christians cannot justify that irrational shift of responsibility. We must not bow without protest before what proves yet another undermining contradiction to the moral fibre of our nation and to the reality of our faith. Far better to tackle the awesome task of reassessing our personal sense of civic responsibility, recommitting ourselves to a biblical definition of righteousness, reconsidering the purpose of our government as defined in our Constitution—and in Scripture—and bringing its costs under control again.

Perhaps, as we consider the magnitude of the task before us, it will strengthen our resolve to do battle, if—in this next chapter—we take a closer look at the way both the governing and the governed respond to the lure of megabucks through some of our more corpulent state lotteries. Don't be surprised if it raises eyebrows!

Points to Ponder

1. Read Isaiah 9:6,7; 22:21 and Romans 13:1. Do these verses suggest that government rests in the hands of

41

God? If so, which concept of government seems more biblical: "government is intended to serve the people, and they bear the financial burden of its function" or "people are intended to serve the government, and it bears the financial burden of their function"?

2. Find the text of the Constitution of the United States in an encyclopedia or at your library and read it to determine what our founding fathers had in mind for the government of this nation? Does government today attempt to go beyond the original proposal to "establish justice, insure domestic Tranquility, provide for the common defence, promote the general Welfare, and secure the Blessings of Liberty to ourselves and our Posterity"?

3. Federal taxes on jewelry and airline travel were among the "temporary" taxes levied during World War II as a means of meeting necessary military budget increases. What quirk of human nature accounts for the fact that those taxes still are imposed more than 40 years after we won the war?

4. If you were called upon to redefine the role of government, what philosophy or concept would you consider most in need of change?

5. When revenue from gambling enterprises is used to pay the cost of government, the burden of supporting that government falls upon the shoulders of those who gamble. Does that suggest the possibility of an inequitable system of "taxation" imposed upon greed, desperation and unrealistic expectations?

4

Making Instant Millionaires

MORE THAN 8 MILLION players held 49 million $1 tickets in New York's 1984 Lotto, then—until eclipsed by Illinois—the richest-in-history state lottery. The pot had sweetened to a total of $22.1 million. Under the ground rules, the money might be claimed by a single lucky contestant or it might be divided between an unlimited number of winners. Everything depended upon the way the numbers fell—if, indeed, they fell at all—and on how many people had purchased those winning numbers.

New Yorkers from all walks of life clamored to get in on the action. People who had never gambled before put a dollar bill on the line—or $10 or $100 or more. A promotional pamphlet urged multiple ticket purchases with its taunting "The more you bet, the bigger your chances of winning!"

No one on the Lottery Board's advertising staff pressed, of course, the equally obvious truth that "the more you bet, the greater your chances of losing." Nor did anyone mention the disturbing fact that state lotteries offer incredibly lousy odds, in spite of the hype that makes them popular pastimes in nearly half the states in our nation.

A Strange Form of Hysteria

Let's go back, however, to the first week of May 1984—a week that made history for New York's lottery program. One TV anchorman described public response to the $22-million pot as "a strange form of citizen's hysteria."

For four straight weeks, no one had held a winning New York Lotto number. When that happens, the prize builds accordingly. The New York pot was $2 million on the first drawing, then $6 million on the second. It escalated to $10 million on the third, and with public frenzy rising to new heights reached an unprecedented $18.5 million on the fourth. By the historical and hysterical weekend in the spring of 1984, the pot had swelled past the $22-million mark.

Lotto Fever! shouted inch-and-a-half front-page headlines in the *New York Daily News.* Pumped-up participants endured hot sun on Friday and chilling rain on Saturday to stand in line for Lotto tickets. Hoards of New Yorkers inched their way along the sidewalks in queues often wrapping completely around the block. Savings accounts and cookie jars were emptied to provide money for wagering. Lotto sales set new records that weekend from one end of the Empire State to the other.

Few, if any, participants complained about the unco-operative weather. Eager investors waited up to four hours, risking sunburn one day and pneumonia the next, to purchase lottery tickets they hoped would make them instant multimillionaires.

The Slimmest of Chances

The chances of winning that fabulous Lotto pot were considerably slimmer than most of the participants realized. What they had to do to win, when the drawing took place that Sunday on the sixty-fifth floor of the World Trade Center, was to pick six numbers between one and 44 in the exact order they would fall. This ordered series of figures is called a "permutation of numbers"—somewhat more complicated than a simple combination. We call it a "combination" when the order in which the numbers turn up is of no importance; it is a "permutation" when each number must fall in the order the numbers are called.

A permutation makes the odds against winning considerably greater than overwhelming. We are dealing here with 44 to the sixth power (44^6). A mathematics professor will explain that you take 44 as a factor and multiply it by itself five times. You might try that multiplication exercise the next time you are tempted to purchase a Lotto ticket—or if you are hooked already.

The Mathematics Department at Miami's Barry University says the odds against winning with any single lottery ticket are 7.25 billion to one. Mathematicians with only eight-digit calculators throw up their hands and suggest it doesn't make much difference. "Just say the odds are astronomical—something close to the national debt," one advised me after exhausting the capacity of his hand-cranked adding machine.

If a player does beat those odds and, if no one else

45

picks his winning permutation, he can claim the prize money, minus federal and state taxes, all for himself—no matter how many millions are in the pot. If a dozen, 100 or more happen to choose his number, he divides the winnings evenly with all the others. Certainly these complications did not discourage multitudes of housewives, taxi drivers, students, clergymen, clerks, laborers, retirees, doctors, bankers—even the unemployed—from bucking the odds in New York's big lottery weekend extravaganza.

A Hot Potato for Evangelicals

The gambling issue suddenly became a hot potato in the state's evangelical churches as hoards of believers broke traditional antigambling ranks and lined up at the Lotto windows. Some explained they would scrupulously tithe their winnings, so as to give God—who owns all silver and gold (see 1 Kings 20:3) along with "the cattle upon a thousand hills" (Ps. 50:10)—"His share." As did others, they came in waves to the ticket vendors to risk whatever money they could scrape together, afford it or not, on the outside possibility they might hit the elusive permutation of numbers and walk away with financial independence for life. Who needs God, some might reason, after that?

On that fateful day in May, the numbers that fell in New York were 36-22-31-3-9-38. Four people held tickets showing the exact winning sequence: a housewife, a machinist, a manicurist and a hospital housekeeper.[1] Their pictures appeared on front pages across the nation.

But exactly 8,137,453 other people with 49,324,868

losing $1 stubs—plus multiplied millions of others who were disappointed in the previous drawings that failed to pay off—did *not* get their pictures in the paper. They were the donors. The $22-million pot of gold divided up by the winners, plus another $27 million or so that went into the state treasury or was paid out for operating expenses, came directly out of their pockets. Some lottery enthusiasts may find this truth elusive, but, as a result of the lottery, these sums of money were not available to the state's economy through normal business channels.

Each winner eventually will receive a total of $5,524,995, payable in annual stipends of $263,095 over a period of 21 years, minus a substantial tax bite that always comes off the top. This method of payment, incidentally, is not the same thing as actually winning $5.5 million up front. The 21-year payoff is a clever device that provides a sizeable fiscal advantage for the state. Given the interest earned on all that money over the payoff period, something like $10 million up front from the lottery treasury guarantees the $22.1 million payoff.

Each of those four New Yorkers, however, has indeed been made rich beyond his or her craziest hallucinations. Promptly resigning from her job as a housekeeper at Benedictine Hospital in Kingston, 64-year-old Weonta Fitzgerald summed it all up with this simple commentary: "I was broke; now I am rich!" By almost any standards, rich is an appropriate word for a person catapulted so suddenly into that formidable tax bracket.

Thinking Christians, however will be concerned that a lot of people, believers included, changed their value systems on that memorable weekend. Millions of New

47

Yorkers and other pot-of-gold seekers who drove across state lines from neighboring areas to join the fun, were converted with a passion to the thrill of suspense and expectation. The bigger the pot grew and the more it was publicized, the more dollars rich and poor citizens alike pumped into the system. On the day before the drawing, 2,300 sales locations across the state reported tickets were being bought at the feverish rate of 17,000 each minute!

That means more than $1 million each hour was spilling out of—not into—New York's economy. Neither product nor service was provided the customer in return for his cash. The final total wagered approached the $50 million mark.

Where the Money Goes

Public records tell us how that money is distributed:

- Of each $1 million bet, $426,000 goes into the New York State treasury, designated for the funding of elementary and secondary school programs.[2] The total take in New York, incidentally, assists the state's school budget by less than 1 percent. That is not what most of us would refer to as a windfall.

- Of each $1 million, $450,000 goes into the pot to be divided among winners, don't forget.[3] That is the rough equivalent, by the way, of 55 percent house "take" in a poker game, a bingo parlor or a gambling casino. No gambler with even a remnant of "smarts" would risk his money against such intolerable odds.

- Of each $1 million, $124,000 goes to administrative expenses and commissions for those who
  sell lottery tickets across the state.[4] Vendors earn
  a nickel for each $1 ticket they sell.

On the momentous weekend in May, New York's
treasury was fattened by $20,900,000. To the average
family-oriented economist that sounds like megabucks,
but to a state treasury it is more like the proverbial drop
in a bucket. From that $49-million total handle, by the
way, administrative expenses and commissions for
ticket vendors gobbled up $6 million.

Where the Money Comes From

State lotteries have no way of manufacturing money
for the special purpose of making those monstrous pay-
outs. Money is not a natural resource to be mined from
the earth, drawn from the air or taken from the sea.
Money is a medium of exchange—a measure of wealth,
assets or value. There is just so much of it around at any
given time. The person who has money got it by fair
means or foul and with or without value received from
someone else.

Citizens who buy lottery tickets pay their money and
take their chance. That chance—the possibility of winning and the probability of losing—is their value
received. The weekly bet, for some, resembles an act of
worship. The lottery state gets those dollars from people
who step forward reverently to pay weekly tribute to the
goddess of good fortune. Her smile, as it turns out, is
reserved for a very favored few.

49

Psychologists who are concerned about the rapidly increasing number of compulsive gamblers in the United States suggest that state lotteries may be generating their own unique brand of addicted high rollers who bet hundreds each week in an irrational and all-consuming search for instant riches. The results often are devastating for families who depend upon these addicts for support.

The Headline Makers

State lotteries develop their own following of unswerving loyalists, and with every big payoff one of those followers becomes a headline maker. Take Mike Wittkowski, for instance, the Illinois Lotto's famous "$40-million man." Mike worked a press for Deluxe Check Printers in Des Plaines before he returned on Sunday afternoon from a week's vacation in Wisconsin to find his life was changed forever.[5] He learned he had beaten the staggering odds Saturday night and landed what still endures as the biggest single-person lottery prize in American history. Mike will have no further use now for that $20,000-a-year job as a check printer. He might, in fact, buy the company. Wittkowski will receive $2 million each year from a 20-year annuity purchased by lottery officials.

Mike is one of those loyal lottery followers. Since he never missed buying tickets, come what may, and since the prize was the biggest in history, Mike instructed his father, Frank, to purchase the ticket for him while he was on vacation. "Put the money on 2-3-10-26-30-43," he said. Fortunately for both of them, Frank stopped by their friendly neighborhood Blatts Drug Store on Chica-

50

go's northwest side and precisely followed Mike's orders.

Not all such lottery loyalists are to be envied, however. Anna May Kelly, of Pittsburgh, Pennsylvania, got her picture circulated by United Press International because she faithfully played the same six Lotto numbers every Tuesday and Friday for two full years. But that loyalty, as it turned out, was not what won her momentary national attention. Fame came her way on the Friday she absent-mindedly forgot to buy her regular tickets.

You guessed it. That is the day her numbers fell, paying more than a million dollars—to someone else. How would you compute the odds against something like that? *Miami Herald* humorist Jay Maeder ran her picture in his column, showing Anna May displaying a handful of no-win tickets dutifully purchased and faithfully preserved through the years. The picture doubtless was furnished by the sly Pennsylvania lottery people who market the program, and Maeder got the message. Under Anna May's picture he commented: "Always remember, young children, someday you might win the Lotto yourself, and it is very important that you continue to gamble away all your money no matter how dark things look."[6]

He Gave His Winnings Away

Then there is Harold Collins of Peoria, Illinois—a $350-a-week engine repairman at the Caterpillar Tractor Company in nearby Pekin—who made headlines twice as a lottery enthusiast. In August 1983, he beat the Illinois lottery for $2.3 million on a $1 investment—this, too, on a 20-year payoff plan. That event turned him into another celebrated winner and installed him in America's lottery legend book.

But nine months later, Collins—who lives alone in a small apartment—was back in the news again. This time it was because he gave his winnings away—every last dollar of it. Why? "I like to work. I like the way I live. I like to watch sports on TV," he told the Associated Press in a telephone interview. "What could I have possibly done with almost two and a half million? I don't need it. I don't do any running around any more, so I got no use for the lottery money."[7]

Because Collins had no use for the money, when his first annual check for $115,276 arrived in the mail early in 1984, he signed it over to Kathy,[8] a happily married South Florida housewife, whom he describes both as "a lady friend"[9] and as "sort of my adopted daughter."[10] Kathy did have use for the money.

Describing their relationship as "kind of complicated," Collins stated that he wed his "adopted daughter" in a marriage of convenience in 1972 when she was 21 and he was 43. But, he added, they never lived together and were divorced three years later.

Oddly, however, Kathy, in an anonymous appearance on NBC's "Today" show, insisted that she and her Peoria philanthropist were never married, that he "has just been like one of the family" for years and that he was simply repaying her for handling his finances ever since she was a teenager. Kathy's husband chose not to comment on the Collins connection.

"I myself don't believe in lotteries," Kathy volunteered to Bryant Gumbel, the "Today" show host.

"Well, if Mr. Collins doesn't want the money, why does he buy lottery tickets?" Gumbel asked.

"Because he's a gambler," Kathy replied. "Collins will gamble on anything."[11]

Her analysis of Collins' character appears accurate. Collins has said he will keep purchasing lottery tickets each week from the same Pekin food store. "And, I'm going to win her again," he announced confidently in a phone interview.

Would he keep the money if he hit it rich again?

"I can't rightly answer that," he said. "No one knows."

Spoken in the true spirit of a dedicated gambler!

But, in view of the almost incalculable odds that Collins and other lottery players face, we might consider "What if you win again" a rhetorical question. Lotteries don't work the way marble shoot-outs or backroom poker games work. In those, the odds—give or take a little, depending on the skills required—presumably are even.

Illinois operates its lottery by the formula common to most states that have legalized lotteries to shore up sagging revenues. Only $45 or so of every $100 generated through Lotto sales is designated as prize money. The rest goes to costs and government coffers. Then there are those odds against getting the right permutation of six pairs of numbers—something like 7,000 million to one.

So don't count on it, Harold Collins. The odds against your winning again probably compare with the number of grains of sand on the beach at Atlantic City or the number of stars over Las Vegas on a clear winter's night!

Points to Ponder

1. Is it true that, in a state lottery, "the more you bet, the bigger your chances of winning"? Might you win more if you bet more? How about your chances of losing? Do you feel a state is keeping or breaking faith with its citizens when it urges them to place bets against overwhelming odds?

2. If the odds of 7 billion to one against you on a $1 bet are reduced to 700 million to one against you on a $10 bet, to 70 million to one against you on a $100 bet and to only 7 million to one against you on a $1000 bet, which bet makes the most sense?

3. Given God's sovereignty and omnipotence, how do you suppose He would respond to a promise to tithe winnings made by someone praying his number will fall in a state lottery?

4. Where does the money come from that is offered in state lottery prizes? When someone wins, who loses? Is a significant part of the money wagered kept out of normal buying/selling circulation, thus harming the economy in the long run?

5. As a citizen and taxpayer, do you accept without question the idea that we must continue to find new ways to get money to pay the ever-increasing cost of government? Why is it increasingly difficult to get that money by increasing our tax load? Why is it that the possibility of winning, even though against incredible odds, can motivate people to donate money to government even when they are unwilling to pay equitably assessed taxes?

Notes

1. *Time,* May 28, 1984, p. 42.
2. New York State Lottery Commission, February 20, 1985.
3. Ibid.
4. Ibid.
5. *Chicago Tribune,* June 12, 1984.
6. *Miami Herald,* May 23, 1984, p. 2.
7. *Miami Herald,* May 23, 1984.
8. Not her true identity.
9. *Miami News,* May 23, 1984.
10. Ibid.
11. "Today," NBC, May 29, 1984.

5
Child of Avarice?

I'LL FLIP YOU FOR IT," may not have been the first sentence Adam uttered to Eve, but the instinct to bet on something, to gamble on the outcome when it could go either way, has been imbedded deep in the human psyche for a long, long time.

I'll lay heavy odds on that!

It may be profitable to ask ourselves, however, to what extent that human psyche can excuse personal indulgences that contain the seeds of our own destruction.

When and where did it all begin? Probably immediately after the Fall, but no one can prove that. Archaeologists have dug up six-sided, dicelike ankle bones of ancient sheep, however, apparently used for gaming at least five millennia ago. With these unusual bones, primitive people probably gambled away long evenings when inclement weather confined them to the family cave. Quite seriously, this historical bit of trivia probably explains the curious synonym, "bones," used today for dice.

Ancient Brahman hymns indicate that great herds of cattle, in what is now India, were won or lost 1,500 years before Christ on the outcome of chariot races. And from all indications, the casting of lots—from which we get our word "lottery"—was part of the tribal life in Asia long before those scattered segments of Mongolian humanity were brought together and given the common designation of "Chinese."

Luck, by the way, has not always been seen as the ruling force when matters were decided by the casting or drawing of lots. Solomon insisted the hand of God was involved. "The lot is cast into the lap; but the whole disposing thereof is of the Lord," he wrote in Proverbs 16:33.

"Lotteries" in the Old Testament Narrative

Scripture provides numerous examples of decisions taken by the casting of lots. In times of national crisis, lot casting was a common occurrence for Israel. Jewish leaders cast lots in Numbers 33:54 to decide which territory each tribe would occupy after the conquest of Canaan. In Joshua 14:2 and 15:1, Moses' successor resorted to the casting of lots in the process of land distribution.

In the account of Achan's swift trial and prompt execution in Joshua 7:14-18, the leaders determined by lot which tribe, then which family, then which household, then which unhappy individual was guilty in the case of the purloined and hidden "accursed thing." The expressions, "which the Lord taketh" and "which the Lord shall take," refer to the casting of lots which quickly identified Achan as the guilty party, and the offending Israelite was stoned and burned along with all his ill-gotten treasures.[1]

After King Saul died, and the full responsibility for leading Israel fell upon David, the "man after God's own heart" (see Acts 13:22) asked the Lord for specific directions in those crucial moments of decision. In 2 Samuel 2:1, "David enquired of the Lord" through the casting of lots and determined thereby that he was to go to Hebron and assume command of the nation.[2]

Consider, also, the important part lot casting played in the life—and near undoing—of Jonah. On his journey to Tarshish by sailboat to avoid an unpalatable assignment in Nineveh, the rebel prophet is found sleeping peacefully in the hold of the vessel. Up on deck, the crewmembers cast lots to determine on whom to pin the blame for a storm that threatened to send all of them to their doom. Sure enough, "the lot fell upon Jonah," (Jon. 1:7). The rebellious ambassador was thrown overboard, the storm subsided, and the rest of the story involving the great fish is a matter of biblical record.

A New Testament Example

The New Testament also contains evidence that in ancient times the purpose of ascertaining the will of God, and not the pursuit of mere chance, was the controlling factor when God's people resorted to the casting of lots to resolve some knotty issue.

Soon after Jesus' ascension into heaven, the 11 disciples who remained after Judas's defection and death gathered in an upper room to select the betrayer's replacement. As they saw it, their choice was between

59

two faithful followers of Jesus: Barsabas and Matthias. The Eleven dutifully prayed, then "gave forth their lots; and the lot fell upon Matthias; and he was numbered with the eleven apostles" (Acts 1:26).

These examples of lot casting from Scripture are not, of course, to be construed as gambling; rather, the casting of lots was a means of seeking God's direction concerning a decision that had to be made. In other words, it was part of a decision-making process.

Gambling as we know it today, addresses more elusive issues of the human spirit. One dictionary defines gambling as "wagering money or other consideration of value on an uncertain event, which is dependent either wholly on chance, or partly on chance and partly on skill." The common denominators are (1) chance and (2) the wagering of something of value. It is the element of chance and the risking of assets that provide suspense and excitement for modern participants in gambling.

How Man Perceives His Environment

Anthropologists note that primitive man's apparent preoccupation with chance probably springs from the way he once perceived his environment—and for some, the perception may not have changed. Artifacts that preserve for us a glimpse of those ancient mindsets hint that the earliest occupants of our planet saw the world as a mysterious arena controlled by gods, demons, monsters, ancestral spirits and other supernatural beings.

Having no knowledge of God, they lived by superstitions, and those superstitions told them that the favor or disfavor of the awesome forces deciding their fate was made known through the unfolding circumstances of life, often through the outcome of chance situations. The revelation might come in a hunt to provide food for survival, in a fight-to-the-death battle with an enemy tribe or in the reckless toss of a sheep's ankle bone for possession of a desirable cave girl or the skin of a mountain goat. Whatever the circumstances, it was assumed that chance was something or somebody out there in the unseen world who either liked or disliked you and who controlled your destiny according to his/her/its whim.

Games of chance doubtless are more formal and better defined these days, but the ancient belief that a lucky gambler is favored by the gods—or by somebody—still persists. In the world of gamblers, superstition still is alive and well.

Gambling Defies the Work Ethic

The upper classes of ancient times tended to associate gambling with profligacy and licentiousness, probably because gambling was thought of then, as in some circles today, as a source of easy money that bypasses the disciplines of professional skill and honest labor. That is in obvious conflict with what we call the "work ethic," still deeply imbedded in most modern cultures. Easy money is commonly regarded as tainted money. During the Middle Ages, rabbis in European Jewish communities forbade all games of chance; Confucius made gambling prominent on a somber list of human weaknesses; Muhammed included gambling among the pleasures forbidden in the Koran.

61

History books tell us, however, that gambling was exploited as an important source of government revenue during the Middle Ages. The city of Florence tried a lottery in 1530; Queen Elizabeth I introduced her English subjects to this novel way of funding government in 1569.

In 1612, the year after the *King James Version* of the Bible was published, James I also authorized a national lottery to raise money for an impoverished Jamestown Colony in the New World, though there is some doubt that the colonists ever saw their share of the loot. The colony and its brave settlers vanished before the funds had time to reach them.

Lotteries Built Churches and Schools

In our earliest national history, colonial legislatures authorized frequent lotteries to raise public revenue before the end of the seventeenth century. Streets were paved, ports were constructed and, yes, churches were erected throughout the American colonies—all paid for or subsidized by lottery profits.

Yale College in 1750 and Harvard College in 1772 raised money for campus construction through public lotteries. In 1776, the Continental Congress vainly attempted to raise funds for the Revolutionary Army by holding lotteries.

George Washington spoke out against wagering— declaring eloquently "Gambling is the child of avarice, the brother of iniquity, and the father of mischief."[3] He also left in his diary a detailed account of his winnings and losses at the card table.

The Uncertain and Unconvincing Voice
of the Church

In spite of a strong Calvinistic influence during our nation's early years, the voice of the Church on the subject of gambling was uncertain and unconvincing. Cotton Mather, the colonial Congregationalist minister, was one of the few clergymen who left a legacy of sermons condemning gambling. For the record, he also supported the Salem witchcraft trials.

Later, Francis Scott Key introduced a resolution in the 1817 General Convention of the American Episcopal Church, deploring the practice of gambling among believers. The composer of our National Anthem characterized the vice as "inconsistent with Christian sobriety, dangerous to the morals of the members of the church, and peculiarly unbecoming to the character of communicants." His resolution, however, was defeated. Deciding such a declaration was not in order "in view of the realities of life," the Episcopal House of Deputies voted it down.

As the Deputies doubtless observed, the Bible is silent where wagering is concerned. The Word of God contains nothing related specifically to gambling. It does, however, denounce greed, slothfulness and worldliness. "The practice of gambling," an anonymous divine wrote more than a century ago, "does not square with the Biblical view of God and the Christian's responsibility to exercise good stewardship." Dr. Preson Phillips of Tennessee Temple University commented more recently, "If God didn't get our attention with His laws about stealing and coveting, He probably felt any reference to gambling would be ignored as well."[4]

Churchgoers, however, are curiously unresponsive to that kind of spiritual reasoning. Pollsters tell us when they survey 10 Roman Catholics, eight of them classify themselves as gamblers. That makes Catholics unchallenged leaders in an ecclesiastical hierarchy of gaming enthusiasts. Not far behind, however are the Jews. Gambling participation among synagogue members is pegged at 77 percent. Presbyterians and Episcopalians are neck-and-neck at 74 percent, with a comfortable lead over the 63 percent of Methodists who admit to gambling tendencies.

Only 43 percent of Baptists surveyed say they gamble, while 33 percent of the members of nondenominational groups, including the traditionally conservative Bible Churches, admit they do a little betting now and then. That figure sounds low when compared to the denominations, but it means that one out of every three conservative Christians may have no scruples against gambling!

The Nation Turns Away from Gambling— for a While

Throughout the nineteenth century, the trend in America was away from gambling. State after state enacted legislation declaring the vice illegal. Louisiana took the nation's final fling until recently with a lottery in 1894, but the venture ended in financial fiasco and rumors of rampant corruption.

When department store mogul and YMCA executive John Wanamaker was Postmaster General under President Benjamin Harrison in 1890, he barred from the U.S. mails "all letters, postcards, circulars, lists of draw-

ings, tickets and other materials referring to lotteries."
For the next half century, that official attitude prevailed.

After World War II, however, the pendulum began to swing the other way, and the public perception of gambling moved again in the direction of the permissive. Churches and charitable organizations turned more seriously to bingo and raffles to raise building and operating funds. Since then, more than 40 states have legalized gambling in one form or another.

As this book goes to press, 22 states, plus the District of Columbia, operate legal lottery programs and others are seriously considering legislation, referendum or initiative proposals enabling them to get in on that financial windfall. It is intriguing, however, that the lottery is found to be licit only when it is operated for the benefit of the state. For any other entrepeneur, gambling still is unlawful. Happy for a new source of revenue—and loathe to propose new taxes—legislators across a broadened spectrum are grappling with the question: If people are going to do it anyway, in spite of illegality and the recognized illogic, why not make it legal *at least for us* and give the state its share of the profits to help solve those budget problems?

Ambivalence in Christians' Perception of Gambling

The chief reason for any citizen's participation in gambling probably is nothing more noble or complicated than greed. There is always the exciting possibility of winning—in fact, of winning handsomely—and most Americans could use an extra dollar now and then. But winning tells only half the story. Losing also is a distinct possibility, and few Americans can handle consistent losses. Yet winners inevitably are outnumbered by losers. In most gambling enterprises, the odds are tilted against the participant and very much in favor of the house or the sponsoring agency. Bucking those odds is not calculated to produce long-term winners.

Unlike other business enterprises, the gambling industry is a nonproducer. It offers neither tangible product nor useful service to its clients and customers. What it does offer is primarily entertainment and recreation in terms of action, excitement, suspense, the possibility of winning and the probability of losing. It brings about a transfer of wealth based not on professional skill, merit, enterprise or other qualities consistent with our work ethic but instead on mere chance and, all too often, on subterfuge.

The public obsession with gambling today raises serious moral and ethical questions for Christians, whatever process of rationalization they may be tempted to follow. Why then, do Christians experience such a strange ambivalence where wagering is concerned? We say, for instance, "After all, we already have betting on horse races, and some people even have bingo in church, don't they?"

Historically, gambling has been included on almost everyone's list of vices, along with prostitution, drug abuse and pornography. So we need to ask: Is a vice different from other forms of crime? A curious aspect of human reasoning is uncovered as we seek next the sobering answer to that question.

Points to Ponder

1. Why do you suppose Solomon and the other writers of Scripture record that the will of God could be determined by the casting of lots? Would you attempt to determine God's will for your life by drawing straws, flipping a coin or some similar means of securing divine guidance?
2. How does the casting of lots as a means of making decisions or choices differ from what we think of today as gambling?
3. According to ancient superstitions, good or bad luck was determined by how ruling gods, demons or other supernatural powers felt about a person. Do you see any resemblance between that mindset and a gambler trying to make his point by throwing the dice while pleading aloud for his numbers to turn up?
4. Do the biblical proscriptions against greed, slothfulness and thievery have any application to the placing of wagers by Christians? Why do you suppose God did not come right out and condemn gambling in some Bible passage?
5. Historically, gambling has been included in most lists of human indulgences to be shunned by responsible citizens. Why do you feel gambling traditionally is classified along with prostitution, pornography and drug abuse as a vice?

Notes
1. "The Lord takes by the casting of lots." *The Oxford Annotated Bible, Revised Standard Version* (New York: Oxford University Press, 1962), pp. 270-271, annotation. "The casting of lots was founded on the belief that God would so direct the result as to indicate His will . . . . It was employed to dis-

cover the wrongdoer in the case of Achan." See James Hastings, *Dictionary of the Bible* (New York: Charles Scribner's Sons, 1937), p. 567. Other commentators express similar interpretations of the Achan account.

2. "Most scholars consider that the phrase 'enquire of God' refers to the Urim and Thummim, which seems to have been of the nature of drawing lots. This occurs . . . in David's uncertainty after the death of Saul." See James Hastings, *Dictionary of the Bible* (New York: Charles Scribner's Sons, 1937), p. 567. "Probably David *inquired of the Lord* by means of the ephod and Urim and Thummim." See *The Oxford Annotated Bible, Revised Standard Version* (New York: Oxford University Press, 1962), p. 375, annotation. Other commentators express similar interpretations of 2 Samuel 2:1.

3. George Washington, Letter, 1783, in *FPA's Book of Quotations* (New York: Funk & Wagnalls Company, 1952), p. 372.

4. Dr. Preson Phillips, phone conversation with author. Used by permission.

6
Deploring and Enjoying Those Vices

How DO VICES DIFFER from other categories of crime? Ask a law enforcement officer—preferably one who serves on your metropolitan vice squad. He doubtless is painfully aware of the subtle difference.

A Crime with Ambivalence

A vice is a crime with ambivalence. In contrast to other types of law violation, it has the added element of enjoyment—of popular appeal and implied public approval or tolerance. It is precisely the enjoyment and the popularity that make gambling a controversial issue in our society—a source of confusion and frustration even for many Christians. And remember, it is an issue that has been with us as far back as recorded history can reach. It is one not likely to disappear from view in the foreseeable future.

Gambling is included among what some call our "victimless crimes," but that inclusion ignores the lost fortunes, the twisted personalities and the ruined lives that are laid at the door of gambling addiction. Nevertheless, it is thought of generally as a "vice."

Murder, rape, burglary, assault and fraud are human activities deemed far less acceptable in the society we share. They are not mere vices; they are out-and-out crimes. They are blatantly immoral in any system of values. They constitute a grave threat to public safety.

Such crimes do intolerable violence to individual security and well being. They are condemned by society and forbidden and punished by law more consistently than are more controversial vices. No one—especially not the victims—could find in felonious murder, rape, burglary, assault or fraud an element of fun or popular acceptance. When we speak of these outrages against humanity, we will not hear amused snickers or see knowing, sidelong glances in response.

We may get those snickers or sidelong glances, however, when we speak of prostitution or pornography or gambling—and the self-conscious snickers and glances are not unheard of among professing Christians. The justification for that discriminating word, "vice," lies in the fact that offenses within those categories—drug use, illicit sex, pornography and gambling—combine *simultaneous fun and wrongdoing* in the eyes of some Americans.

Deplored By Some; Enjoyed By Others

Apply a realistic definition to vice, then, and you speak of a human activity that can be deplored by some people while it is being enjoyed by others. Human nature being what it is, the deploring and the enjoying may even be done at the same time and by the same people! That is why "vice laws" often are not enforced as stringently as those making other more overtly dangerous or intolerable human behavior illegal. Even if they are enforced, the penalties are less harsh. Some Americans would like to see all of them repealed.

Seldom do you hear of a campaign to legalize murder, rape or bank robbery. The proponents wouldn't get very far. But a sizable segment of our society would like to take the illicit stigma from those prohibited—though enjoyed—human weaknesses we refer to as vices. "After all, everybody does it anyway," is the rallying cry. Powerful forces are at work today contending that no one should be allowed to set arbitrary rules to govern the behavior of others. Legalized gambling, pornography, marijuana, cocaine and prostitution have proponents in the society all of us must share.

When Vices Become Licit

We are confronted by a curious paradox whenever new legislation changes an activity traditionally regarded as a vice from criminal to legal. The stigma is removed, but the suspicion and the fears remain. Moves to legalize gambling inevitably resulted in the placing of strong bureaucratic control over those allowed to provide the legalized gambling opportunities. The industry that previously was illicit is expected to accept the necessity of those controls. But seldom does it work out that way. As soon as the enterprise is declared legal, its entrepeneurs begin to regard themselves as legitimate businessmen. They resent and inevitably resist the state's attempt to "control" them.

When Nevada repealed all laws against gambling in

71

1931, it anticipated the need for controlling agencies to protect its citizenry from the potential evils of the industry it had declared legal—legal, yes, but not really trustworthy. The nature of that control has evolved through the years, and it must continue to change in response to increasingly shrewd efforts by the casino industry to elude its restricting hand.

The Only Thing Different Is the "Legal" Label

The new label of "legal" did not, of course, change the character of Nevada's potentially threatening public indulgence. Neither does God's righteousness or His will for His people change along with public sentiment or bow to a majority vote. Gambling itself remained exactly whatever it was before the legalizing took place—in Nevada, as anywhere else. The character remains the same; the classification of "legal" is the only thing that is different.

Nevada's carefully designed control apparatus, however, bears eloquent witness to the fact that those who benefit from the liberalized laws can be counted on to abuse their privileges. That reservoir of anticipated abuse includes not only the lingering likelihood of infiltration by organized crime—with all the evils it can perpetrate upon society—but also skimming of profits, evasion of taxes and felonious rigging of odds beyond an acceptable level to help the house fleece the unsuspecting gambler. Now and then, the roles are reversed and it is the gambler who fleeces the house. It becomes a simple strategy of "doing unto others before they do unto me!"

The necessity of a controlling agency and rigidly restrictive guidelines where gambling and other vices have been made legal clearly implies that the once-prohibited-but-now-legitimized activity still is dangerous. Though it now bears the *imprimatur* of public acceptance, it retains nevertheless a proven potential for inflicting harm upon society. Restricting laws and controlling agencies clearly imply: "Where there is vice—legalized or otherwise—someone must be on guard to protect the public interest."

The Paradox of Legitimized Gambling

So here is a paradox: in the light of these implications and the fears of public harm, how do we justify the legalization of, say, a state lottery in Montana or gambling casinos on Miami Beach by claiming the indulgence isn't really all that dangerous? Where is the moral and spiritual spine in passing it all off as inevitable "because people do it anyway?" I find roaches in my kitchen now and then, but I'm not importing more of them or throwing away my Raid.

How can we hold that vices offer benefit to society and need not be feared, yet maintain at the same time that they are illegal unless they are done by the state or under its control? If they are harmless, then what is the justification for those strict controls? Our desire to protect ourselves lays bare a precarious and untrustworthy side to the industry which we legalize in spite of the calculated risk.

To decriminalize a once-recognized vice and then to say the enterprise is legal for no one but the state or the privileged few it authorizes will be seen, sooner or later, by protest groups as another new area of hypocritical discrimination. By the time our anarchists think it through, state lotteries and carefully controlled casinos doubtless will become yet another invitation to violent dissent.

The Question Is: Do We Choose to Participate?

The question is not whether we will consent to live in a society where integrity is elusive, where abuses are widespread and where winning or losing valuable assets depends on the toss of a coin, the finish of a race, the turn of a card or the fall of a bingo number. Christians are not in the majority, and we do not control the democratic process. The question is whether or not it is in our own best interest as followers of Jesus Christ to participate in a potentially harmful vice, simply because the state legalizes it and society describes it as "merely having fun."

In many states, our co-existence with legitimized high rollers has been determined for us already through the inevitability of human weakness and the fluctuating ethics of our society. But being in the world does not make us proponents of the world's priorities or participants in its value system. For centuries, Christians have accepted in triumph and by faith their unique role of sharing the environment with worldlings—yet remaining aloof from and uninvolved in their follies.

Legal or illegal, approved or disapproved, wise or unwise, harmful or otherwise, betting on something and hoping for the impossible apparently is a permanent character flaw wherever members of the human species are found. In this particular swing of the pendulum, opposition against lotteries and casinos is crumbling. The moment may be close at hand, in fact, when believers who voice their opposition against gambling will be classified as holdovers from the days of chaperoned dates and segregated dormitories.

Let me show you a dramatic example of that human character flaw as we see it in action at 49 oval tracks across our nation. So let me take you where the "King of Sports" reigns before a court of frenzied spectators holding $2 tickets to win, place or show—but mostly to lose.

All set? Then let's get going.

Points to Ponder

1. Is gambling really a "victimless crime"? Even if the family breadwinner cannot be classified technically as a compulsive gambler, are his dependents deprived by his losses at the race track or card table?
2. As a Christian, suppose you were asked to select the "least sinful" indulgence among the following: (a) attending an *XXX*-rated film at an "adult" theater, (b) spending an evening with a prostitute or (c) betting at a roulette table in Las Vegas? By what criteria would you determine your answer? Do you think God maintains a rating scale for sins as we are prone to do?
3. Does it trouble you that in states where lotteries have been legalized this kind of wagering still is illicit and

punishable under the law *except* when it is sponsored by the state? Is there something about state sponsorship that takes away the stigma of "wrong" and provides an ethical and moral acceptability for something otherwise considered criminal?

4. What is implied by the fact that where casino gambling has been legalized the state creates rigid laws and guidelines to monitor and restrict the way the industry conducts its business? If casinos are harmless, why the suspicion on the part of the authorities and the imposition by them of strict controls rather than relying on the good old American "assumption of innocence"?

5. If a Christian determines that indulgence in gambling is, indeed, contrary to the will of God for his life, which of the following courses of action would make the most sense: (a) leave no stone unturned in a personal campaign to rid the world of gambling temptations; (b) discuss with your pastor and church officials the possibility of a church rule prohibiting members from placing bets; (c) make a quiet personal commitment to the Lord that, with His help, you will avoid situations that might lead to your being tempted to indulge in the vice?

7
Running for It

HORSE RACING CAN be viewed from two dramatically different perspectives, and anyone aspiring to understand the insidious power of the "King of Sports" will not have a complete picture without knowledge of both of them. One point of view is concerned with *racehorses;* the other is concerned—perhaps "obsessed" is a better word—with *horse racing.*

Neither side gets its kicks exclusively from cashing in win, place or show tickets or even from pocketing prize awards. Mere day-to-day involvement in the racing world somehow appears to provide sufficient seduction and excitement to make the investments of both the owners and the bettors seem worthwhile.

A few racehorse farms fortunate enough to breed or buy consistent winners or own a sought-after stud do manage a profit, but the general consensus is that average racehorse owners usually end each year substantially in the red. Almost certainly, the average racetrack wagerer does. An important difference is that the wealthy owner probably doesn't worry about his losses.

If he had to, he wouldn't be indulging himself with those unpredictable and outrageously expensive animals in the first place.

The World in the Stands and the World in the Stables

Just as marked is the difference between the racetrack's up-front world in the stands and its behind-the-scenes world in the stables. The former is inhabited by customers lining up at the betting windows or cheering favorite horses down the homestretch. Hidden from sight in the stable area is a bivouacked world always on the move and perpetually on the make.

The horse himself is unchallenged emperor of this busy kingdom—and many of the presumably dumb beasts actually appear to savor their status. If the horse is rightly described as king, then his court and his legions are composed of multitudes of assorted hangers-on: jockeys and jockeys' agents, exercise boys, hot walkers, clockers, grooms, trainers, vendors peddling alfalfa and 60-gram horse aspirin, and—inevitably—stereotypical characters eternally in search of a tip.

Those "tips" seldom provide the promised winner, but they form the bridge to the up-front world that springs suddenly to life with the shout, "They're off!" The hottest tip on today's races begins to circulate at 6 A.M. when the behind-the-scenes world comes alive, but by noon that same tip has faded to a lukewarm status, and by starting time it probably has been discredited altogether—replaced by new rumors someone heard that someone else overheard in conversations between, say, the trainer and his jockey.

The barns below are in rows, and the stalls inside the barns also are in rows—but there are never quite enough stalls for all the entries. The first thing most visitors notice about a racetrack stable probably is the flies. They are everywhere—most notably pestering the horses, resting in windowsills and perched precariously on hanging bridle pieces. Next come the smells. The mingled sweet-sour aroma of liniment and manure permeates the atmosphere around the stables and a hundred yards beyond. That distinctive odor battles for supremacy with the smoky smell of bacon (for the people) frying in the stable kitchen, and oatmeal (for the horses) cooking in giant tubs.

Barn areas have their own peculiar sounds too: metal gates clanging, tails swishing and hooves stomping in the stalls, strident voices shouting orders to stubborn mounts, shrill protesting neighs, leather bridles slapping and horseshoes clicking on the cement or blacktop pavement. That is the unique ambience of the racehorse world. It creates a strange sort of enchantment for those who make it their home.

A Contagious Disease Loose in the Horse Race World

The atmosphere of the stables is a far cry, however, from the ambience of the horse race world. What is happening in the stands is even more obsessive than what is happening behind the scenes. Grim-faced bets at the ticket windows, followed by frenzied shouts at horse and jockey beside the oval track is a routine that is dangerously contagious. Life up-front at the races appears to find its ultimate meaning at betting windows and finish line.

The horse race world revolves around a paper called the *Racing Form.* The form's readers make up one of the world's most dependent and loyal followings. "If I had spent the time studying law books that I've put into the *Racing Form,*" an aging attorney at Belmont[1] was heard to lament, "I'd probably be on the Supreme Court by now."

The *Racing Form* occupies the place in the life of the horseplayer that the Bible is intended to occupy in the life of a committed Christian. For the genuine race-track devotee, it is the source of all knowledge and the basis for all hope. Its incredible reservoir of information on horses and their performance record is the stuff from which life's most important decisions are made for the unhappy man or woman hooked on the races. Its code-like symbols and the handicapping principles that incorporate them provide all the guidance the sophisticated bettor requires.

There is, indeed, a highly developed science of hand-icapping, but few ever master it and prove their mastery by their consistent winning. Yet a working knowledge of the handicapping system apparently makes the princi-pal difference between the amateur and the professional at the racetrack betting window.

Computers Decide the Odds When You Bet

Because the betting dollar at the racetrack is so heavily taxed under the pari-mutuel system,[2] those who wager on the horses—or the dogs—have little chance of winning consistently. Computers calculate odds constantly as bets are placed. They automatically determine, according to formulas established under state law, how much a $2 bet can win on each horse to win, place or show. The computers determine how much from each purse goes to the track, how much goes to the state and how little goes to the bettor. The rare wagerer who does win probably is one with both the superior knowledge and the superior persistence required to perfect the art of analyzing and interpreting the *Racing Form*. An occasional touch of good luck, too, is considered an ingredient of more than passing importance.

Horse racing columnist Andrew Beyer begins his *Picking Winners: A Horseplayer's Guide* with the warning: "From time to time, every confirmed horseplayer is racked by doubts about what he is doing with his life. He is playing the toughest game in the world, one that demands a passionate, all-consuming dedication from anyone who seriously wants to be a winner. Even a winner will necessarily experience more frustrations than triumphs, and when the frustrations come in rapid succession he may wonder if the struggle is worth it."[3]

The Lure Is Greed

Beyer contends that most horseplayers are lured to the racetrack primarily by greed. All but mesmerized by autosuggestion, they believe what is whispered to them by tipsters and system peddlers and make their contributions at the ticket windows with almost unshakable confidence that they will win. A never-ending stream of how-to-beat-the-races books convince them there is easy money to be made at the track.

Beyer points out that consistent winning would require a series of almost incredible strokes of good luck, since, under the pari-mutuel structure, the various racing states and the tracks claim from 15 percent to 20 percent of every purse. In the simplest possible terms, what that means is that more money is bet than can be won. Horse racing, like dog racing and—in Florida—jai alai, is tightly controlled and heavily taxed under the pari-mutuel formula. That makes the majority of bettors inevitable losers.

"It is a testimony to the unique lure of racing," Beyer writes, "that once a man has discovered it and starts losing money . . . he usually doesn't abandon the sport and put his capital into municipal bonds."[4]

Horse racing expert Walter Haight used to advise his friends, "When you're betting on the horses, be sure you think of your money as if it were chips or marbles or whatever else you might use to keep score and determine how well you are doing. You can't let money become anything more than a symbol. If you ever start thinking about money as something you could use instead to make a mortgage payment, retire a debt or buy a car you'll start having anxiety attacks and discover the truth of the old saying, 'scared money never wins.'"[5]

We Must Live with Reality

Reality cannot be banished that easily, however, For most of us, the more important functions of money include buying the necessities of life for ourselves and for our dependents, providing a bit of security for our declining years and bearing our fair share of the cost of the work of the Lord. Habitual wagerers usually are negligent in one or more of those responsibilities.

Even highly touted "betting systems" eventually prove unreliable, though they are as varied and as imaginative as they are unsuccessful. The fact that the parimutuel system skims off for the state one dollar out of every five dollar bet is a powerful system breaker in itself. But on top of that the bettor must reckon with all of the unpredictables and the foibles of racing animals and the people who exploit them. His horse—or dog at the "kennel clubs"—may falter in the starting gate, be bumped in the turn, fall in the stretch, devour the rabbit or become the victim of dirty tactics by an overzealous competing jockey. The wagerer, in spite of his allegedly brilliant personal handicapping[6] system, could even be cheated out of potential winnings by deliberate fraud—such as when a jockey is instructed by the horse's owner to hold his animal back and lose the race so the odds will be greater the next time when he runs against lesser competition. Life is full of such surprises for those whose focal point is the oval track.

The Syndicating of Horses

On the *racehorse* side, the proliferation of super farms for breeding and boarding these animals has encouraged the expansion of what horse people call "syndication" of thoroughbreds—an investment strategy that can skyrocket the value of a stud horse of exceptional ancestry almost overnight. The plan is relatively simple: everyone who purchases a share in the proven stud can use the horse to service his own mares and produce racing stock. Outsiders, in some instances, may "buy in," but they pay dearly for the privilege.

83

Syndicated thoroughbreds now and then continue to be entered in races—and even to win purses for the shareholders—but the principle reason for the investment strategy is the availability for stud services to shareholding farms or the selling of those services to others. This sale of services can continue for years after the horse is too old to run but not too old to follow his natural reproductive instincts.

One of the reasons for the stratospheric value of thoroughbred horses is that all of them must descend from an incredibly exclusive family line. The rules for qualification are uncompromising. All animals competing in organized flat racing must be listed in the official national stud books or registers of their countries. The British stud book was begun in 1791; the American book was created in 1873. A horse is not acceptable in the ranks of thoroughbreds unless his ancestry can be traced—literally—to three animals that were imported into Ireland and England from the Middle East at the beginning of the eighteenth century. That means thoroughbred horse breeders are dealing in a very rare commodity indeed, and those who wish to share in the benefits must pay dearly for the privilege.

The Need for Strict Control

The racehorse and the horse race industries are sanctioned and strictly governed today by the Thoroughbred Racing Association, which came into being in 1942 and which has developed a stringent code of standards aimed at encouraging a high level of ethics in racing. The necessity of a controlling agency came on the heels of long-tolerated shenanigans at the track and a resulting reformist sentiment early in this century that resulted eventually in the outlawing of bookmaking, and thus racing itself, by all our states.

With the advent of pari-mutuel systems—computer control that determines odds and fair shares based on the betting in each race—in 1930, however, 49 major tracks in the United States and seven in Canada were legalized. They quickly proved major sources of revenue for the sponsoring states—and, of course, for racetrack owners as well. Again, the bookmaking that had been declared illicit suddenly became legal once more, but this time under altered circumstances. The legal acceptance applies only if betting is done under state-controlled systems that presumably protect the average American. These systems are intended to prevent us from being exploited by entrepreneurs who now are declared law-abiding citizens—though not as trustworthy as, say, someone who owns a hardware store or teaches junior high school students for a living.

Make no mistake about it: Americans are captivated by the idea of betting a little and winning a lot. If they cannot find one way to pursue that fantasy, they will dream up another. And for many in pursuit of their "big win" instincts, their dream come true—their ultimate fantasyland—is hitting the jackpot in a casino. Yet what about casinos? What really lies behind those glittering facades? Is the world of legalized casino gambling all its backers claim it to be? Or is there more to it than meets the eye? Let's take a look and see for ourselves.

1. What do you suppose accounts for the electrified atmosphere at a racetrack during the two minutes a group of horses gallops around the oval track? Is the suspense based on "Which horse will be victor?" or on "How much money will I win?"

2. How does the pari-mutuel betting system differ from the kind of wagering that takes place in a gambling casino or in an illegal bookmaking operation? Does computer control make fraud and corruption in the betting less likely?

3. What are some of the factors in horse racing and dog racing that deny even veteran racetrack wagerers, in spite of elaborate handicapping and betting systems, any guarantee they will come out ahead?

4. Syndicated thoroughbreds often earn for their owners prize money totaling much more than what was paid for them—sometimes millions of dollars. How does this kind of revenue differ from win, place or show bets at the racetrack window?

5. Suppose you were observing the activity at a racetrack and you saw your pastor; someone you regarded as a truly fine Christian; perhaps a renowned Christian leader such as Billy Graham, Pat Robertson, Robert Schuller or Jerry Falwell; maybe the Pope, for that matter, plunking down his money at the betting window. Would you be surprised? Disappointed? Cynical? Critical? Pleased? Strengthened or weakened as a believer? Why would you react in that way?

Notes

1. "Belmont" refers to the Belmont Park racetrack in Elmont, New York. Three races each year—the Belmont Stakes, the Kentucky Derby and the Preakness—together comprise thoroughbred racing's "Triple Crown." To win these three events in a single racing season is the most sought-after accomplishment in the U.S. horse racing world.

2. A "pari-mutuel system" is "a betting pool in which those who bet on competitors finishing in the first three places share the total amount bet minus a percentage for the management." "Pari-mutuel" also refers to the "machine for registering the bets and computing the payoffs in pari-mutuel betting." *Webster's Ninth New Collegiate Dictionary* (Springfield, MA: Merriam-Webster Inc., Publishers, 1985), p. 856.

3. Andrew Beyer, *Picking Winners: A Horseplayer's Guide* (Boston: Houghton Mifflin Co., 1975).

4. Ibid.

5. Ibid.

6. In racing parlance, a "handicap" is "a race or contest in which an artificial advantage is given or disadvantage imposed on a contestant to equalize chances of winning; and advantage given or disadvantage imposed usually in the form of points, strokes, weight to be carried, or distance from the target or goal." "Handicapping" then is "to assess the relative winning chances of (contestants) or the likely winner of (a contest)." And a "handicapper" is "one who assigns [such] handicaps" such as "one who predicts the winners in a horse race usually for publication." *Webster's Ninth New Collegiate Dictionary* (Springfield, MA: Merriam-Webster Inc., Publishers, 1985), p. 550.

8
Atlantic City and the Abrams Report

ROBERT ABRAMS FAVORED legalized casino gambling when he became Attorney General of the State of New York in January 1979. Casinos already had come to Atlantic City, and he was favorably impressed. Controversial as the casinos might be, they were generating significant tax revenue for the state and municipality that had sanctioned them. They were responsible for the apparent rejuvenation of a once-popular tourist haven that enjoyed a glorious past and faced a dubious future.

New York State needs additional revenue as much as most other states, and Abrams was well aware of the heavy political responsibility he and other incumbents bore to find a solution. The entire nation knew of the financial roller coaster traditionally ridden by New York City, and many Big Apple citizens felt legalizing casinos, even in a limited area somewhere in Manhattan, could provide a bailout source capable of solving the city's fiscal problems for years to come. Some Christians were adopting a hands-off attitude, rationalizing that gamblers would gamble whether the rest of society liked it or not, and why not get all that tax money for the state and relieve the overburdened taxpayer?

But Abrams reasoned that revenue for the city and the state must not be the only consideration. He knew other factors must be weighed and other areas explored before the Empire State could consider whether or not casinos would be in its best interest. So he began asking questions and listening to a mind-boggling mixture of answers.

Enthusiasm Wanes with a Closer Look

"I must admit that my enthusiasm began to diminish with closer scrutiny of the issue from the unique perspective of my new office," the Attorney General wrote.[1] To assemble information that would assist the State Legislature in reaching a decision about casinos, Abrams assigned staff members to conduct an intensive study of the advantages and disadvantages of casino operations in both Nevada and New Jersey. Meanwhile, Governor Hugh Carey had appointed a Casino Gambling Panel to conduct an inquiry for the state, and Mayor Edward Koch had commissioned John F. Keenan to submit to the city a report on casino gambling. Information from both these studies also was made available to the Attorney General.

For six months, Abrams and his staff searched myriads of records and files for facts and statistics. They conducted lengthy interviews with those who favored casinos and with those who opposed them. They were looking for facts, not opinions or passions. Out of this investigation Abrams experienced a growing concern.

He invited Attorneys General from several northeastern states to visit Atlantic City casinos with him and to interview law enforcement officials in this newly created arena.

"As a result," the New York Attorney General writes in a landmark anticasino document known as the *Report in Opposition to Legalized Casino Gambling in New York State* (Abrams Report), "I became increasingly well acquainted with the numerous facets of this complicated issue."[2]

One Man's Bonanza; Another Man's Agony

And complicated it is, because what is perceived as one man's bonanza can just as easily emerge as another man's personal agony. Strong opinions are encountered on both sides, and the emotional issues involved make it difficult for some opinion holders to be objective. The huge sums of money at stake for the gambling industry suggest that the rational basis for its claims, ethically and pragmatically, at best should be viewed as shifting sand.

Abrams' disenchantment with casinos as a solution to the state's financial dilemma appears to have been slow, cautious and, in a sense, reluctant. He wanted to find a workable solution to New York's budgetary problems as much as anyone. Yet, having gone to considerable pains to search out available facts and implications, he was unable to deny the reality of his findings.

Crime, Criminals and Corruption

"Revelations in 1980 of a myriad of problems associated with New Jersey's casino gambling industry—in particular, the soaring rate of casino-related crimes in Atlantic City and recurring allegations of organized crime infiltration and influence peddling at federal, state and local levels—were, for me, the final straw," Abrams' report explains. Then he summarizes his conclusions with this categorical statement: "I am now persuaded that casino gambling in New York State would not be in the public interest."

"Specifically," Abrams writes, "I believe that the financial and economic benefits to be derived from passage of any of the eight resolutions to legalize casino gambling now before the Legislature are outweighed by the added crime and the corrosive and disruptive effects that legalized casino gambling is likely to have on communities where casinos are located and on the people and institutions of our state."[3]

The Abrams Report lists three major factors the Attorney General credits with reversing his opinion about the acceptability of casino gambling:

> 1. The evidence from Nevada and Atlantic City that conclusively indicates, according to investigators, legalized casino gambling will be accompanied by a debilitating upsurge of crime in the areas where the casinos will be located.
>
> 2. Gambling casinos are considered a magnet for organized crime.
> 3. Legalized casino gambling poses a danger to the integrity and credibility of government institutions and public officials.

The single-spaced, 24-page Abrams Report carefully documents these three caveats. In public records readily accessible in Atlantic City and Trenton, as well as in the casino oases in Nevada, considerable justification for Abrams' concerns can be found. His pessimistic prognosis seems confirmed by what he terms "irrefutable evidence of enormous crime problems in the two areas of the United States where casino gambling has been legalized: Nevada and Atlantic City, New Jersey."[4]

Nevada: Undisputed Leader in Crime

Nevada has had more than half a century to learn to derive all available benefits from casino gambling. That historically adventuresome frontier state legalized all forms of gambling in 1931. But the gains have been offset by significant losses. During those 50-plus years, according to the Abrams Report, Nevada has become undisputed leader in crime statistics in the United States. In Las Vegas alone, 36,000 serious crimes are recorded each year, and the figure continues to rise. With approximately 100 murders annually, *Las Vegas has the highest per capita crime rate of any city in our nation.*

"There are 10,000 prostitutes active (in Las Vegas)," *U.S. News and World Report* noted in 1981.[5] That number equals one out of every nine women in Las Vegas between the ages of 15 and 39—though those age limits for inclusion in "the world's oldest profession" admittedly are arbitrary! Law enforcement officials generally agree that the correlation between prostitution and casinos is easily recognizable.

Nevada, by the way, is the only state in the nation

that has de-criminalized prostitution. "People are going to do it anyway," the electorate has reasoned. A bumper sticker in keeping with current trends and uniquely appropriate to that avant-garde state might read, "Nevadans do it legally!"

A Staggering Crime Wave

The most convincing statistics suggesting a direct cause-and-effect link between casinos and local crime come from Atlantic City. The first casino, Resorts International, opened there in May 1978. Shortly after that historic event, the city began to experience what the *Atlantic City Press* described as "a staggering crime wave in the wake of casino gambling."[6] During 1977, before the opening of Resorts International, Atlantic City's total crime index stood at 4,391. In 1978 it rose to 5,738, and by 1980, with six casinos in operation, the crime rate had skyrocketed to 11,899.

That's a 170 percent increase.

In contrast, during the same three-year period the overall crime rate in all of New Jersey increased by only 26 percent—with the Atlantic City statistics factored in as the chief cause of the increase.

Across the Spectrum
from Muggings to Murder

According to the official Uniform Crime Reports of the New Jersey State Police, these figures reflect increases in murder, forcible rape, robbery, aggravated assault, burglary, larceny and motor vehicle theft. That

94

provides a well-rounded picture of violent acts against the lives, safety and well-being of New Jersey's citizens and the city's guests. A 1986 study by the Florida Department of Law Enforcement concluded that the introduction of casinos into Atlantic City "was paralleled by a significant increase of criminal activity."[7]

The skyrocketing of pickpocket complaints is a good example of problems created by the sheer mass of humanity crowding Atlantic City. During the new gambling mecca's formative years from 1977 to 1980, such complaints soared from 15 to 544!

Given the unique circumstances, that particular statistic should be no surprise. When the vulnerable citizen presumably is on his way to the casino to lose it all anyway—or, is homeward bound with easy money gained by merely picking a lucky number or drawing the right card—an unscrupulous individual with sticky fingers would experience few, if any, scruples against relieving him of his poke. "Street thugs—drawn to the people and the money—saturate the avenues leading to the casinos and the public parking areas," reported the *Atlantic City Press* in 1980. "Visitors unfamiliar with the city wander a block or two off the beaten path and are attacked."[8]

In another report, the newspaper warned, "People are getting mugged almost as soon as they get off the bus at the Atlantic City Bus Terminal. Many of those who get safely through the terminal become victims of crime on their way to the casinos."[9] These are statements of newspapers intent upon the propagating of objective truth, not of religious or moralistic alliances desperate for arguments against a foe predetermined to be culpable.

Casinos Create a Poisoned Atmosphere

Most of Atlantic City's street crime appears to be imported. It is brought into the city along with the games. As one police official explained it, "Crime just sort of goes with the territory—it's a part of the atmosphere casinos create." Atlantic City police say 95 percent of those arrested for crimes against persons or charged with car theft are out-of-towners.

Narcotics deals reportedly are made routinely on the busiest of Atlantic City street corners in broad daylight. According to an article in the *Philadelphia Inquirer,* anything can be purchased along certain streets near the Boardwalk, "from heroin to cocaine, methamphetamine to stolen cars and television sets."[10] One local police official described the social impact on the citizens of Atlantic City as "devastating."

A Stockton State College study of casino-related problems of Atlantic City's senior citizens disclosed that elderly residents of the area are prime targets for criminal attacks in their homes as well as on the streets. In the South Inlet section, Jewish senior citizens have been attacked on Friday evenings while on their way to their synagogues—indeed, even robbed inside their place of worship.

"Alienated from the Life of God"

That kind of environment may be acceptable to worldlings, but it is foreign and unacceptable to Christians. The redeemed are to "walk not as other Gentiles walk, in the vanity of their mind, having the understanding darkened, being alienated from the life of God through the ignorance that is in them, because of the blindness of their heart . . . past feeling . . . given . . . over unto lasciviousness . . . uncleanness with greediness" (Eph. 4:17-19).

The erstwhile thief is admonished to "steal no more . . . working with his hands the thing which is good, that he may have to give to him that needeth" (v. 28). We are warned that no "covetous man, who is an idolater, hath any inheritance in the kingdom of Christ and of God" (Eph. 5:5). Gambling casinos tend to create their own environment, with covetousness, greed and worship of the Goddess of Chance as the central theme.

A Desert of Urban Blight

Robert Alsop, respected *Wall Street Journal* writer, visited Atlantic City and wrote that the casinos are "lush oases in a desert of urban blight." He concluded his story with the statement, "The deterioration is like a cancer."[11] That cancer is metastasizing rapidly, reaching deeper and deeper into the political body of America.

The Casino Control Commission reports that more than 50,000 juveniles attempt to get into Atlantic City casinos during summer vacation months, and that at least 10,000 of them succeed in reaching the gaming tables. A student counselor at Atlantic City High School told the State Assembly's Institutions Committee that an increasing number of students play hooky to gamble at the city's casinos. He claims students as young as 14 manage to gain admittance—in spite of required ID checks—and many leave their lunch money in the slot machines.

In early years arson figured prominently in Atlantic

97

City's casino-related proliferation of criminal activity. Presumably because the now-valuable land was coveted by speculators for casino development, several once-proud residential districts of the city were ravaged by fires of suspicious origin—peaking at nearly 50 alarms each month until most of the choice property was gone. Finally the incidence of arson returned to normal, since there is little more that can profitably be burned.

If these horror stories have the ring of overkill on the part of forces hostile to casino gambling, remember that most of these facts surfaced through a study authorized and supervised by the chief law enforcement executive of the State of New York, a man with no axe to grind. Other allegations are gleaned from reports by responsible journalists seeking to inform their readers of the facts.

The Greed Money Generates

Proponents of legalized casinos almost invariably seek to focus our attention on mind-boggling sums of money and on the greed money generates. Yet the fact is that few, if any, benefits are produced by the casino industry beyond the dazzling megabucks potential they claim to represent: jobs, tax money, better schools, better health care and a prosperity shared by all. At best, these alleged benefits are the broken promises of a deceptive crystal ball; at worst, they are deliberately and feloniously designed to mislead a greedy and gullible public into providing unscrupulous entrepeneurs with an incredible financial bonanza.

Results from Atlantic City's all-or-nothing fling with gambling still are inconclusive, but one side of the issue

98

is shockingly clear: a staggering amount of money can be siphoned from the pockets of America's gamblers via proven formulas developed by the casino industry. "What remains unclear," cautions an editorial in the *Asbury Park Press,* "is how the unprecedented casino revenues ... can be used to fuel redevelopment of a dreary city that still looks a lot like someone forgot to tell it what's going on."[12]

Faced with a 2,000 percent increase in demand for its services because of the increase in crime since the legalization of casino gambling, Atlantic City's police department, according to the Abrams Report, has been unable to cope with the problem. State officials and newspaper editorial writers alike have leveled charges of poor police administration and departmental turmoil. Hints of bribery and other corruption surface frequently. Abrams' investigators brought to light reports of reluctance on the part of state police to share with city police sensitive information regarding gambling and drugs. State law enforcement people blamed that on what they termed suspicious relationships between local police officials and Atlantic City numbers rackets kingpins.

An Atmosphere of Suspicion

This atmosphere of suspicion could be at least a contributing reason many of the city's most experienced police officers have resigned their positions to accept more lucrative security posts with the casinos. That attrition, too, is a troublesome factor that helps multiply law enforcement budget and efficiency problems in Atlantic City.

"The actual Atlantic City and Nevada experiences

have conclusively demonstrated to me," Attorney General Abrams writes, "that legalized casino gambling, by its very nature, creates an environment in which crimes of all types will flourish . . . . I believe it is too high a price [for New York State] to pay for the economic and financial benefits of casino gambling."[13]

Particularly unsettling are the Abrams Report's statements concerning the inevitability of organized crime's involvement in the cash-producing and cash-laundering potential of casinos.

"There has existed and continues to exist an incestuous relationship between the casino gambling industry and organized crime," Abrams writes. "It is an historic and deep-seated union, nurtured by the vast amounts of money involved in casino gambling and by the extraordinary opportunities which casinos, and the environments in which they flourish, offer for organized groups to engage in a wide range of illegal and lucrative activities."[14]

Al Capone Never Had It So Good

The almost unbelievable amounts of money generated by casinos today exceed by far anything Al Capone could have dreamed of in the heyday of his Chicago booze monopoly. The annual "gross win" of Atlantic City casinos already had reached $623 million in 1980. By the next year, the amount exceeded $1 billion.

While "gross win" is a term accepted in the industry, it is just as accurate—and a trifle more sobering—to refer to those megabucks as only part of the "gross gambler loss." Casinos are not allowed to print money or import it from outer space to be handed over to occasional jubilant winners, though it may appear that way occasionally on the gaming floor. Whatever the house awards in prizes—overshadowed by the staggering amounts it posts as profits—must come from the pockets of disappointed players who lose more than they win.

The "gross gambler loss" in 1985 was more than $2 billion. That means patrons of Atlantic City's casinos leave behind an average of $5.5 million *each day*—and that's in addition to what they spend for lodging, meals, travel and whatever personal indulgences may seem desirable.

"The size, nature and amounts of money generated and spent by the casinos draws the criminal toward the industry," says G. Michael Brown, director of New Jersey's Division of Gaming Enforcement. "It also makes the casinos more vulnerable to illicit schemes and more susceptible to extortion plots."[15] Casinos are not just faceless, soulless fun-and-game machines; they are business enterprises owned by corruptible human investors who emphatically are in it for the money.

The Pressures and Tensions of the Industry

As the man primarily responsible for law enforcement and policy implementation when casinos first came to Atlantic City, Brown understands the enormous economic pressures imposed upon these businessmen who must—according to a Resorts International vice president—gross *half a million dollars each day* from all casino-related sources in order to break even. Brown knows the intimidating power that unions can wield over such an industry through threats of strikes by a broad spectrum of hotel and casino workers. These sources of possible tension range from croupiers to bellboys to bartenders to garbage collectors.

Brown also is aware of Atlantic City's unsavory past during mobster Angelo Bruno's almost undisputed reign for a decade or more over the area's lucrative vice enterprises. He witnessed the deterioration of the gang's control during the underworld violence of 1980 and 1981, when competing hoodlums murdered five members of the Bruno family in an effort to muscle into their territory.

All That Goes with the High-rolling Life

Visitors to gaming cities like Las Vegas, Reno and Atlantic City are not searching exclusively for recreational gambling opportunities. Many are looking also for the goods and services that are identified historically with the high-rolling life: drugs, bookmaking, loansharking and prostitution. Who is better qualified or more pleased to furnish these lucrative services than the unscrupulous organized crime figures homing in on those megabucks?

Criminals are strongly motivated to attach themselves to the casino industry, and man-made devices to block them rarely are effective. "The Family" accomplishes this not only through peripheral ancillary services, loan-sharking and money-laundering schemes but also through hidden ownership and movement into top management posts and key gaming positions.

Skimming Methods in Casinos

True to its watchdog instinct, the Internal Revenue

Service conducted its own investigation into what it terms "Casino Unreported Income" and found five major categories where suspected skimming of profits takes place. These are (1) kickbacks to owners, (2) fictitious operating expenses actually pocketed by managers or owners, (3) fictitious gaming losses similarly misappropriated, (4) fictitious cash advances and (5) manipulation of accounts receivable. The IRS report states that "False billing, gaming losses and cash advances have long been used as skimming methods in Nevada casinos."

Former New Jersey Attorney General John Degnan testified before a committee of his state's legislature on March 3, 1980, and described vividly how he viewed the involvement of organized crime in Atlantic City. He declined to comment when he was pressed to reveal specific evidence of infiltration of casinos by known criminals, but proceeded to ask and answer the questions he felt should be of primary concern to committee members:

"But is organized crime present in Atlantic City? Yes. Is it there in greater force than it was before casinos were passed? Yes. Are they trying to buy liquor licenses? Yes. Are they trying to get into ancillary industries? Yes. Is there an increase in prostitution? Yes."[16]

Degnan added that loan-sharking and bookmaking have increased sharply since the first casino opened in Atlantic City, and he blamed that on organized crime. Later, he told the Eastern States Attorneys General Conference in Newport, Rhode Island, that organized crime connections have been traced to real estate transactions in Atlantic City and also in the infiltration of casino-related unions.

103

Organized Crime Can't Be Filtered Out

It is a naive assumption that regulatory procedures can filter out or prevent the involvement of organized crime. Those charged with implementing the precautionary codes do not always invoke the measures prescribed. Three Atlantic City casinos were licensed by the New Jersey Casino Control Commission, despite opposition from the office of the state's Attorney General. The opposition was based on alleged business transactions by the applicants with reputed organized crime figures, but the commissioners were unconvinced that this was grounds for a denial of the license.

The Abrams Report terms "illuminating" the case of Bally's Park Place Casino, which received its license on December 29, 1980, along with a ruling that its founder and chief executive, William T. O'Donnell, was not qualified to hold a license. The commission based its objection on O'Donnell's history of association with reputed organized crime figures and on his alleged participation in a scheme to bribe Kentucky legislators in 1968.

O'Donnell testified before the commission that "some [of his] past associations have been dubious," but he characterized these as "mistakes in judgment" and requested the commission to reconsider. In this case, it declined.[17]

Substituting a "Front" for the Banished Corporation

The Attorney General argued that the company's association with criminals was so flagrant that the Bally organization—whoever might be its titular head— should not even be allowed to sell slot machines in New Jersey. A history of subterfuge was reviewed in support of the objection. In 1975, the Nevada Gaming Commission had ordered Bally to sever all ties with a vending machine distributor who had underworld connections. In compliance, according to the Abrams Report, Bally merely substituted another company which was allegedly a front for the same disreputable organization.

When the Nevada Commission ordered Bally on another occasion to disassociate itself from a Louisiana gaming machine distributor who had been convicted in federal court on racketeering charges, Bally is reported by Abrams to have transferred its business to another partnership made up of the convicted man's five children.

Infiltrating Casino Unions

At the time the Abrams Report was published, law enforcement agencies had grown fearful mobsters would gain control of the gaming industry by infiltrating the casino unions. They were closely monitoring an effort by the Teamsters Union to organize dealers from the casinos' poker tables. They also reported a struggle among unions with underworld ties to organize the casinos' security personnel. Casino Police and Security Officers, Local 2, with headquarters on Long Island— allegedly affiliated with New York's notorious Gambino family—had gathered enough signatures to mandate elections at three casinos in Atlantic City.

The office of the Atlantic County Prosecutor is quoted in a *New York Times* story as saying, "Based on what we have seen, the most likely target for monopolistic control by organized crime of a significant segment of the casino economy would be through these unions."[18]

That fear may be well founded. The Senate Permanent Subcommittee on Investigations concluded in August 1984 that organized crime wields "substantial influence" over the 400,000-member Hotel Employees and Restaurant Employees International Union (HEREIU). After a three-year probe, the subcommittee reported that organized crime's control is particularly strong in the huge locals in America's gambling meccas. "Numerous officers and employees have documented ties to organized crime figures, and there is little doubt that Local 54 (Atlantic City) is now controlled, and Locals 226 (Las Vegas) and 30 (San Diego) have been influenced in the past by organized crime interests," the panel reported.[19]

Payroll Padding and Cronyism

Mismanagement of the enormous sums of money that accumulate in union benefit funds particularly intrigued the Senate's investigators. "The membership has been cheated by an international union payroll padded with associates, relatives and cronies of top HEREIU officers and persons associated with organized crime," the report reads.

Union president Edward T. Hanley and six other union officials "seriously obstructed" the work of the subcommittee by refusing to answer questions while invoking their constitutional rights against self-incrimination, the panel charged.

106

In a written response to the allegations, HEREIU officials denied any connection with organized crime and charged that the panel's probe "was not a fair and impartial inquiry into the union's operation." It would have been surprising, indeed, had the HEREIU leaders owned up to the charges and calmly accepted the consequences.[20]

The union branded the work of the Senate investigators "a premeditated effort on the part of the subcommittee to destroy the reputation and credibility of the union and its officers." HEREIU said that for the subcommittee to criticize its officials for invoking the Fifth Amendment "is to criticize the Constitution itself." It claims investigators "relied upon unauthorized [Justice Department] leaks . . . innuendo . . . convicted felons, admitted perjurers, psychopathic liars and thoroughly discredited witnesses."

As some astute observer of human nature once put it, "A strong offense is the best defense!"

The State's Limited Power to Regulate

New Jersey's Division of Gaming Enforcement has attempted to disqualify at least one union because of suspected associations with organized crime figures. Local law enforcement people have been reluctant to pursue this strategy vigorously, however, because they fear they may find they have only limited powers to interfere in the affairs of labor unions. Because the unions are regulated by the United States Labor Department, there is room for doubt that they can be made subject to sanctions by the state's regulatory agencies. Thus the observation of a *Trenton Times* editorial that,

"The mob has targeted the unions as the easiest point of entry into the Atlantic City casino industry."[21]

Lt. Col. Justin J. Dintino was Chairman of a New Jersey ad hoc committee assigned to seek possible organized crime links through casino credit applications and complimentary services records. He has testified that casinos welcome big-time criminals as gaming customers because they are good for business in two important ways: the mobsters often are high rollers themselves, and more than that they have good connections that lure other desirable customers to the tables.

Dintino has identified four potentially dangerous practices of the casinos that make them vulnerable to known criminals:

1. Each of the city's nine casinos has routinely extended credit and provided complimentary services—such as free rooms, meals or other more intimate services—to known organized crime figures and their associates.

2. By obtaining easy credit at the casinos, mobsters have been able to turn that credit into immediate cash, which they can then use to finance loan-sharking, narcotics trafficking and other criminal activities.

3. Reputed crime boss Nicodemus "Little Nicky" Scarfo and other organized crime figures allegedly have received VIP "comps" from several casinos without going near the gaming tables.

4. Joseph Pedula, a Bruno crime family associate indicted in New York for the gang-style execution of Salvatore Testa and described by

Dintino's investigators as a "paid contract killer," was allowed to deposit more than half a million dollars in cash in a private account with Resorts International Hotel and Casino— an account that enabled him to deposit or withdraw cash in large sums at the gaming tables as a privileged client.[22]

As Dintino points out, the establishing of private accounts makes it possible for criminals to launder illicitly obtained money. "If you rob a bank and feel like the money is hot," he writes, "what better way to launder it than put it up as front money at a casino. When you come back several days later to get it, you won't get back the same money you came in with."[23]

The Exclusion List Is No Deterrent

The State of New Jersey does publish an exclusion list, which identifies known crime figures and presumably prohibits them from entering casinos. Few officials consider the list an effective deterrent, however. According to Dintino, the list does not, in reality, prevent mobsters from showing up regularly on the casinos' floors. His committee identified numerous known organized crime figures who routinely patronize casinos in Atlantic City as well as in Nevada. After a random sampling of more than a half-million casino credit and "comps" records, the committee identified 37 known racketeers and their associates who were allowed credit by the casinos, and who received complimentary services because of their value as "high rollers."

In the spring of 1980, revelations of influence peddling and official corruption in New Jersey rudely awakened the public to the extraordinary power of the casino industry to contaminate the political process and to influence government at all levels. In one Abscam incident, the vice chairman of New Jersey's prime regulating and licensing body, the Casino Control Commission, resigned after disclosure by federal authorities that he had not reported a $100,000 bribe offer. Allegedly, he was promised that sum in cash if he helped a fake Arab organization purchase land to build and operate a casino.

The Abrams Report documents several similar incidents which illustrate convincingly the lamentable truth that the megabucks of the gaming industry too often can control the very regulatory process designed to keep it in line.

When Everyone Has His Price

The cynical observation that "everyone has his price" may not always be true in terms of cold cash, but organized crime knows other means of persuasion. Where bribes fail, the hoodlums know alternative ways to make their illicit schemes prosper. A public official who cannot be purchased for $100,000—or even for a million—might consent to almost anything in the face of a hint that his wife might be disfigured by acid or that his children might not make it home safely from school.

"There's no telling any more who is really regulating whom," complains an editorial in the *New York Times.* "The casinos simply have too much money to make and spend (for us) to avoid the legal corruption of government."[24]

The Abrams Report points out that "more than 50 local officials and government employees in Atlantic City own stock in casino gambling companies, or have been involved in the purchase or sale of property for casino use, or have other financial links to the casino gambling industry. These include the police chief, a city commissioner who once was deputy police chief and the City Commissioner for Public Safety.

Five of the nine members of Atlantic City's Planning Board have been identified by the Abrams Report as having either invested in or had property or financial dealings with the casino industry. Members of the two boards responsible for key zoning decisions allegedly have routinely been involved in land deals with the casinos and have personally benefitted from casino-related transactions approved by their own boards. With this kind of data on record, the confidence of the public in the regulatory boards established to protect its rights sinks to a discouragingly low ebb.

Everyone Gets Part of the Action

Dozens of Atlantic City employees, including police officers, housing commissioners, budget personnel and deputy mayors, have flocked to the employ of the casinos. The Director of the Casino Hotel Association, according to the Abrams Report, once was the Director of Atlantic City's Housing and Urban Renewal Authority. In that position of public trust, he helped negotiate the sale of two urban renewal tracts to casinos. The Director of the city's Planning Board suggested to a casino development corporation how it could bypass requirements of the city's master plan prohibiting use of a particular

111

site for casino development—then went to work for the company. Several former state legislators with connections and influence at the highest levels of government have been hired by the casino industry for a variety of responsible and well-paying positions.

"The casino industry's seductive nature and efforts to buy influence are further demonstrated," insists the Abrams Report, "by the fact that influential state and local officials throughout New Jersey have been offered special privileges and courtesies by the casinos in Atlantic City. This led former Attorney General Degnan to label the industry as 'inherently dangerous because of its propensity to curry official favor.' The Chairman of New Jersey's Joint Legislative Committee on Ethical Standards has commented: 'Is this whole industry going to continue wheeling and dealing in politics? . . . it is a disturbing pattern, and not what the public agreed to when it voted to try casino gambling.'"[25]

What Do People Expect from Casinos?

What, in fact *does* the public agree to when it votes to "try casino gambling"? Deborah L. Choban of Miami Beach, Florida, eloquently stated the rationale of those determined to "save" her financially troubled community when she authored this statement for the "Readers' Forum" page of the *Miami Herald.*

"To restore Miami Beach to what it once was," the determined lady wrote, "we should legalize casino gambling. This would spark tourism and provide more employment. Contrary to popular opinion, casino gambling does not breed crime or disrupt our normal way of life. Instead, the casinos would help to control crime in the streets to protect their image. The taxes collected from legalized gambling would pay for education, fighting crime, transportation, social services and health care."[26]

What more could anyone ask? Our needs for education, law enforcement, public transportation, social services and health care will be provided through an industry we may rest assured—against all the evidence to the contrary—neither breeds crime nor disrupts the local citizen's normal way of life. In fact, we are reassured that these benefactors can even be counted on to help control crime in the streets—so great is their desire to protect their image from tarnish. We can enter with confidence into a new age of urban recovery and individual prosperity—or so we are told. All these benefits are handed us without cost or obligation by benevolent forces getting all that money from sources which need be no concern of ours!

Casinos Through Rose-Colored Glasses

Bennett Lifter, who is prominently identified with the move to legalize casino gambling on Miami Beach, offers this summarization of the advantages casinos would provide, as he sees it, for local citizens—but most of all for the 500-room Marco Polo Hotel which he owns:

"All Floridians are concerned about jobs and a better economy, so that it behooves them to have gambling, which makes hotel operations more profitable, leading to creating more jobs, more construction, and more usage of services and supplies, which benefits the entire area. Also, more jobs, of course, get the people, including a large number of blacks, off the streets and reduce

113

the rate of crime," he writes. And the proof he gives us?

"This is proven," Lifter adds, "by Atlantic City, which has become the No. 1 vacation destination of the world, with a great deal less serious crime than has been publicized by the media."[27]

If you believe that, I have a nice, only slightly damaged, building in Beirut I'd like to sell you! Like others who stand to profit most from the casino trade, Lifter sees what he *wants* to see when he peers into his crystal ball.

The hotel owner sees casinos, in fact, as a solution to the crime problem, not as a contributing factor. "The crime in Florida primarily consists of drug traffic," he writes. "More jobs and better economy would lessen the need for illegal businesses. A healthier economy would lead to less tolerance on the part of the community toward drugs and other questionable type businesses that are accepted to some degree by the community as a need of economic necessity."[28]

It must be assumed, of course, that hotel owner Lifter has been exposed, as we are, to the Abrams Report and other studies in conflict with his point of view. Given his personal interest, however, he prefers the more palatable message he gets from his own balance sheet. What is in the best interest of our nation, it would appear—like beauty—is indeed in the eyes of the beholder. And not many are beholding in deference to the Lordship of Jesus Christ.

Points to Ponder

1. Casinos have been described as "rivers of cash, with many strange animals coming to the water to drink." Do you see any correlation between this uncharted flow of megabucks and what Robert Abrams refers to as the inevitability of corruption of some local officials?

2. Opponents of casinos see the Abrams Report as a sort of Magna Charta in the citizens' campaign to brand these "leeches licensed to prey on the false hopes of the foolish" as what they really are: legitimized rackets that know in advance just what percentage their "take" will be. What have you seen in this overview of the Report that gives you food for additional thought in establishing your own point of view where casinos are concerned?

3. Everyone is said to "have his price." Is there a sense in which that might apply to even the most faithful Christian? Suppose someone with neither scruples nor conscience—and fully capable of fulfilling his threat—told you he'd see to it that your spouse or children would meet with some tragic fate unless you responded to his unlawful demand? Would that demand become, in fact, your "price"?

4. The casinos in Atlantic City lure thousands of people each day to their gaming rooms, bringing them from surrounding cities in huge busloads. Each person pays $20 for the bus ride and, in return, gets a $3 lunch ticket and $15 to gamble with. How can casinos make money on a deal like that? Is it possible

they know in advance just how much of his own money the average bused-in customer is going to gamble away once he gets there?

5. A wealthy personal friend of the author who once owned a famous casino denied the category of "gambler" for himself, saying, "Casino owners don't gamble; they know they're going to get their percentage, whatever happens." Is there any sense in which the casino customer similarly can know he is going to emerge a winner?

6. Honestly, do you think you would experience a certain amount of embarrassment if Jesus Christ returned to earth and found you placing your chips on the squares of a roulette table? If He asked you for an explanation, what do you feel might satisfy Him?

Notes

1. State of New York, Office of Attorney General, *Report in Opposition to Legalized Casino Gambling in New York State,* 20 May, 1981, prepared by Attorney General Robert Abrams, p. 1. This document is subsequently documented as the Abrams Report.
2. Ibid., p. 1.
3. Ibid., p. 2.
4. Ibid., p. 2.
5. *U.S. News & World Report,* March 9, 1981, p. 66.
6. *Atlantic City Press,* December 22, 1980.
7. State of Florida, Florida Department of Law Enforcement, Investigative Analysis Bureau, *Casino Gambling Update,* May 1986, p. 1.
8. *Atlantic City Press,* December 22, 1980.
9. *Atlantic City Press,* November 12, 1980.
10. Quoted in the Abrams Report, p. 5.
11. *Florida Times-Union* (Jacksonville), November 23, 1981.
12. "Impact," *Asbury Park Press,* January 1, 1984, p. 5.
13. The Abrams Report, p. 7.
14. Ibid., p. 8.
15. G. Michael Brown, speech delivered at the Maryland Public Gaming Research Institute, Baltimore, MD, March 17, 1981.
16. *New York Times,* March 23, 1980.
17. The Abrams Report, p. 13.
18. *New York Times,* December 1, 1980.

19. U.S., Congress, Senate, Permanent Subcommittee on Investigation, *Report of the Permanent Subcommittee on Investigation,* 16 August, 1984, p. 3.
20. *Miami News,* August 27, 1984, p. 1.
21. *Trenton Times,* February 4, 1984.
22. *Trenton Times,* March 6, 1983.
23. Ibid.
24. *New York Times,* editorial, June 19, 1980.
25. *New York Times,* November 30, 1980.
26. *Miami Herald,* letter to the editor, August 28, 1985, p. 12.
27. Response to questionnaire from author, written reply, January 18, 1985.
28. Ibid.

9

An Inside Look at Casinos

BEFORE WE LEAP to conclusions based wholly upon the Abrams Report, let me take you inside a gambling casino for a more intimate view of what enthusiasts experience after they pass through those ornate doors.

When Resorts International learned of my plans to write a book on gambling trends in America, its management reasoned the author's research ought to include a personal visit where the action is. They invited my wife, Diane, and me to spend four days as their guests on Paradise Island in the Bahamas, and—in the interest of objectivity—we accepted. I will share in this chapter the insights developed during that visit.

After a one-hour flight from Miami in an amphibian of Chalk's International Airlines, Inc.—also owned by Resorts International—checking in at the exclusive Paradise Club removes any lingering doubts as to what this posh Bahamian tourist attraction is all about. The VIP player whose personal wealth or high-roller status entitles him to such accommodations quickly finds himself surrounded by special privileges seldom seen at run-of-the-mill luxury hotels.

An immaculately groomed concierge, carefully selected on the basis of brains, beauty and—doubtlessly—discretion, accompanied Diane and me to our eleventh floor hideaway. We represented, of course, neither wealth nor status but received our special treatment through the generosity of hosts who prudently asked no questions about what we intended to write.

The Word Here Is "Gamble"

The focal point on this narrow strip of land just across the channel from Nassau is not the luxury, however, and neither is it the gourmet delights in a dozen different restaurants, the lure of a Professional Golfers' Association golf course, the awesome spread of tennis courts, the submarine rides, the parasailing or the variety of fun and games on the beach. When you walk through the impressive portals of Paradise Island Resort & Casino, you know you have come to gamble.

Resorts International bills itself as "the most complete island resort in the world," and the claim may not be exaggerated. Everything the visitor needs to make his stay complete is available inside or adjacent to the complex. It is close enough to downtown Nassau to provide whatever souvenirs or adventure the vacationer might require. It is also isolated enough to provide a sense of seclusion and single-minded devotion to the primary purpose that brings him here.

When Diane and I entered the cavernous 20,000 square feet of gaming delights known as "the casino," we walked first through what seemed acres of slot machines—thoroughly modern 25-cent and $1 electronic devices that provide a major portion of the casino's revenue. These are the first, simplest, fastest and most reclusive ways of gambling available to patrons. Many gamblers never get beyond the slots.

Sticking with the Slot Machines

"It's just me against the machine," one middle-aged lady told us. With a look of grim determination, she fed the insatiable apparatus a diet of quarters from a paper cup generously furnished by the house. She was not contending with a dealer or a croupier—or even with other players.

That evening she was sticking with the slots that take five quarters at a time—straight across on three lines and two more lines at angles, like bingo. She likes the idea of being able to play the slot machines any time she wants to. "I like to take a shot at 'em right after breakfast," she explained, speaking in a detached way as she inserted her coins and pulled the handle with an authoritative flourish. The slot machine area is always open, day and night, while other games are closed from two in the morning until noon.

Now and then the lady hit a combination of symbols that returned a few of those quarters and replenished—for the moment, at least—her depleted supply of coins. "But they always get 'em back in the end," she sighed, as she dropped another $1.25 and pulled the lever yet again. She starts each day of fun and games with $25 worth of coins. That day they "lasted quite a bit longer than they usually do—it must be my lucky day." Her $25 stake had provided her with almost half an hour of excitement but, as she looked sadly at the dwindling supply of quarters, she realized the fun soon would be over unless she made another trip to the cashier's window.

"I really ought to quit when the cup is empty," she said somewhat sheepishly, "but somehow I always end up going back for more quarters. This (bleep) thing has been known to pay off as much as $250 at one time—but it always pays it to someone else!" She reckoned her losses at "maybe $100 a day—it's more fun if I don't keep track too closely."

The Hefty Progressive Jackpot

The progressive $1 slot machines pay off the most generously—taking more, of course, in return. A computerized device registers each $1 slug placed in a selected group of machines and adds 5 percent of that amount to a progressively larger pot. The bonanza will be handed the first person who hits the winning combination of three bells straight across. It is a long, long time between bells. The exact amount in the pot at any given moment is displayed in lighted red digital numbers directly over the machines. There had been no winner for weeks.

That day the progressive jackpot had swelled to more than $126,000, so Casino Operations Director Dennis O'Brien reduced the 5 percent to only 2 percent. "No point in letting the pot get much bigger," he observed.[1] Each player pictures himself walking out with that 126 grand, so eager investors stumble over one another to deposit their money in the dollar slot machines.

Intensity at the Blackjack Table

A few yards away, and still within earshot of the clattering, whizzing and clinking of the slots, are the blackjack tables—the scene of what appears to be the most intense contests in the arena. Here it is each player against the dealer, and there is always the possibility that skill in remembering what cards already have been dealt will increase the player's chances of being hit to a winning 21.

That "21" is the name and the object of the game, and that's the number dealer and players alike try to reach. After the players place their bets on the green felt cover, the dealer gives two cards—faceup—to each player and two cards—one up and the other down—to himself. Face cards count 10, and other cards count whatever number they show. Aces can count either 1 or 11, whichever is needed at the time. The player counts his numbers and makes swift calculations in his head. He must decide whether to stand on what is showing or draw to increase the total of his cards without exceeding 21.

If his two faceup cards show a total of, say, 15, then he knows if he draws anything up to a six it will bring him closer to the winning total of 21. On the other hand, if he calls for another "hit" and happens to get a seven or above, he "breaks" and his chips are lost. The inscrutable odds always are against him, but he is here to challenge chance, not bow to reality.

House rules require only the dealer to draw if he has up to 16 and to stand if he has 17 or above. But because one of the dealer's cards still is facedown, the players don't know what he has and therefore don't know how close to 21 they must come to beat him. The dealer completes his hand after the players have called for their hits and either broken or decided to stand.

If the dealer breaks, then all unbroken players win. If the dealer stands, say, on 18, then anyone who shows more than that wins, and anyone who has less than that loses. A tie is a standoff—nobody wins. For the dealer to handle all the cards and the variety of players' bets swiftly and accurately requires a sphinx-like concentration and a microchip calculator for a brain. He is paid well, but he is also watched with secret-service intensity by a sharp-eyed pit boss who must answer for any slip-ups on his shift.

Roulette: Favorite Pastime of Aristocrats

The game that characterizes gambling casinos more than any other is the roulette wheel—long among the favorite pastimes of European aristocracy. Today it has multitudes of enthusiastic devotees among growing numbers of casino sophisticates on this continent as well.

Roulette's big attraction centers in the spinning wheel, the bobbling ball and the variety of wagers it offers. Add to that the fact that it can provide the excitement of a large payoff on a relatively small wager—often enough, at least, to keep the player's juices flowing in hopes the big win is coming with the next turn of the wheel.

The 38 numbers, including 0 and 00, that appear around the circumference of the roulette wheel also are stretched out before the player like a hopscotch pattern on a green felt board—along with combinations like "black" or "red," "odd" or "even" and various groupings of numbers. The player may choose a single number—which pays 35 to 1, 2 to 6 numbers, 12 numbers or 18 numbers in as many combinations as he has chips to cover. He does this by "straddling" the table numbers with his chips. He can make, as the casino's gaming guidebook puts it, "many other fascinating betting combinations."

Craps, Baccarat and the Wheel of Fortune

The dice table has such a plethora of rules that newcomers to the casino often are frightened away from the game. Many linger to watch, however, and Diane and I soon were straining our necks with other spectators. We pondered a vast array of betting possibilities on the long sunken craps table, with choices like "pass line," "come" and "don't come," challenging the player to take his choice or to forget the whole thing. There are "hardways," "one-roll bets," "horn bets" and "any craps." There are the numbers themselves and the "no call bets" and the "don't pass bar."

Craps tables are generally regarded the scenes of the fastest action and the most noise in the casino, and the tables at Paradise Island are no exception. If dice had ears, they would hear a repetitive chorus of loud and insistent performance commands—or prayers—with every throw, as players call for a number to fall so they can win their bets. Only one player at a time can throw the dice, but the number of bets that can be placed is almost unlimited. On busy nights, players crowd around the long table, with spectators bringing up the rear.

The baccarat—pronounced *bah-ka-rah*—table is in sharp contrast, but we dared not intrude for a closer

125

look. Baccarat usually is installed in a remote corner of the casino, and kibitzers are not allowed. While dice throwers, blackjack patrons and roulette players are clad in sport shirts, shorts and blue jeans, baccarat players wear jackets and ties—often even formal dresses and tuxedos. The impression is that baccarat boasts the quiet, thoughtful and quality players who move in casino circles with more aplomb than ordinary tourists can muster.

The least complicated of all the casino games is the Big Six Wheel—informally called the "Wheel of Fortune." The player puts his money on the number of his choice any time before the wheel stops turning. Numbers circle the wheel with various odds up to 40 to 1 on "joker" or "paradise." The higher the odds, the fewer the chances that the wheel will stop on that number. Only one such slot is provided on the wheel's perimeter for a 40-to-1 win, with considerably less than a 1-in-40 chance that the pointer will stop there.

"Casino Owners Never Gamble"

In order to turn a profit—which is, of course, their reason for existence—casinos must operate on scientifically determined and easily controlled odds formulas. Given enough time and play, the games provide their owners—though not, on purpose, the players—with a generous return on their investment. A former casino owner told me, "Casino owners never gamble. We know we'll get our 15 percent no matter who gets lucky or who folds."

Now and then someone takes home a sizable pot, but that never frightens casino managers. They know

126

they will get their money back—if not from him, then from someone else. What is called "luck" involves only the occasional win while the numbers are adjusting themselves. For every big winner, there are losers who drop even more. Losers return to recoup their losses—only to lose again. Winners often end up handing their money back to the casino in a futile effort to win even more. The owners know they can count on greed to even the score.

When a player gets truly involved in wagering, his perceptions undergo a mystical and radical change. The money invested in chips no longer symbolizes to him what it symbolizes to nongamblers. Whether he can afford it or not, he will shove a thousand dollars worth of wheel chips onto the roulette board, watch them evaporate into thin air and shrug off a loss that would cause acute anxiety for someone not under the hypnosis of the game.

Money Is a Stewardship Responsibility

To most people, money signifies confidence, security, promise and well-being, not only for themselves but also for those who depend upon them for the things money will buy. As Christians, we see in money specific stewardship responsibility by which we declare ourselves involved in what God is doing on Planet Earth. We work hard to get money, plan carefully how to use it efficiently and try to put aside as much of it as possible against the unforeseen demands sure to tap us on the shoulder a few furlongs down the road.

We grumble over unexpected expenses and complain when people charge us more than what strikes us

127

as fair. We agonize over the unwelcome task of balancing bank statements and celebrate when the miscalculation this month is in our favor. We rejoice in bargains and chortle over those rare strokes of good fortune which put a little unexpected cash in our pockets. We see in $5, $10 and $20 bills symbols of how much effort it took to acquire that purchasing power, and how it can grow and serve us and our Lord, if we treat it with respect and appreciation. Seldom, however, are we privileged to so much as hold a $50 or $100 bill in our hands.

Money: the Stuff That Keeps the Action Going

That is not true, however, of high-rollers at casino gaming tables. Money means something else to them—at least while they are handing $100 bills to the cashier or shoving their chips toward the croupier at the roulette table. What the money symbolizes metamorphoses when it enters the casino. It no longer signifies confidence, security, promise or well-being, and it certainly has no connection with the work or the will of God. Gambling dollars no longer represent stewardship responsibility, purchasing power or the future meeting of creature needs. Money and chips, to the gambler, are merely the stuff which keeps the action going—like make-believe hotels, railroads and utilities in a Monopoly game. As long as a little of the fantasy remains, the game can and must go on.

"Yes, greed plays an important part in keeping people coming back to our tables," Dennis O'Brien acknowledged.[2] In fact, keeping them betting and losing and coming back to lose again has been the name of the casino game since "Bugsy" Siegel in 1943 persuaded his crime syndicate he could transform Las Vegas into a legal oasis for organized crime and a source of incredible bundles of the stuff that keeps the action going.

An Uncomfortable Alliance

It took an uncomfortable alliance between this eastern mobster and the straight-laced Mormons of southern Nevada to make it happen, but by 1945 Siegel had his Flamingo in operation in the largely unnoticed seat of Clark County—until then distinguished primarily by its aboriginal Indians and its copper mines.

Operating then out of Beverly Hills, California, the cagey Siegel figured he could count on huge profits from his legalized games, but he also knew it would take more than dice and roulette wheels to lure customers away from Reno's combined attractions of gaming rooms and quick divorces. He accomplished that by providing the most beautiful and least chaste women, the most luxurious accommodations, the finest food and wines and the most celebrated Hollywood entertainers—all at such reasonable prices few could ignore them. It didn't matter what the frills cost; profits at the gaming tables would more than cover the loss.

Siegel may have forgotten, however, that he was using someone else's money, and his shadowy backers were increasingly irritated with his high-handed ways. When the mob gets irritated, it has a disturbing tendency to eliminate the cause of that exasperation. In due time, Siegel was targeted for a "hit," with the single stipulation that the "icing" should take place somewhere other than in Las Vegas. The gambling mecca's reputation as a peaceful town must be protected at all costs— and it was. Siegel was gunned down in his mistress's Beverly Hills mansion in 1947. He should have stayed at home.

Siegel's death, in fact, created an air of intrigue for Las Vegas which doubtless attracted thousands of customers to the casinos. Today some tourists still visit Las Vegas in hopes of rubbing shoulders with gangsters. The fact is, if they did they probably wouldn't know it. Mafia members don't wear name tags, and they don't necessarily don felt hats, smoke big cigars and speak with Italian accents. Bugsy's Flamingo now is owned by the Hilton Corportation.

Inadequate Control of the Games

Until Siegel opened his Flamingo, gaming control in Las Vegas had been the responsibility of local and county officials. The 1931 state law that legalized gambling had established county license fees based on the number of games operated, and assigned county sheriffs, district attorneys and committees of county commissioners as licensing authorities.

It soon became evident, however, that such controls were inadequate, particularly in the light of the cunning and the lack of scruples among the people who were involved in the industry. A new 1945 Nevada law, then, moved this authority to the state, requiring licenses from the state tax commission and levying a tax of 1 percent of gross earnings.

When mob figure Frank Costello was shot to death

in New York 10 years later, and figures for gaming revenue at the Tropicana Hotel were found in his blood-soaked pocket, it became clear that state-imposed controls still had failed to screen out unsavory hidden interests and that no amount of legislation could ensure the exclusion of undesirables from a share in casino profits.

Only two years earlier the Nevada Tax Commission had found a flaw in the ownership records of the Thunderbird Hotel in Las Vegas, and the state had brought suit to suspend the casino's license. The Attorney General contended that Jake Lansky, brother of alleged underworld financial genius Meyer Lansky, was one of the hidden owners. Lansky had made a huge loan to the owners of record to finance hotel construction, and the state saw in that loan a not very subtle effort to mask his interest as part owner.

The state lost the case. Nevada's Supreme Court declined to uphold the license suspension order, and Lansky and the Thunderbird went their merry way. Defense lawyers presented a convoluted argument to prove that the hotel and the casino were separate entities, and the court ruled that Lansky—clearly ineligible for casino involvement because of his documented crime connections—did not actually participate in the gambling enterprise.

The Sticky Fingers of the Mob

Nevada and New Jersey continually restudy and strengthen their casino control apparatus to guard against the involvement of organized crime, yet the effectiveness of such controls inevitably is questionable.

Too many dollars are at stake and too few scruples intervene to permit measures sufficient to keep the nimble fingers of the mob out of the cookie jar.

The length and dexterity of those fingers were confirmed during the summer of 1983 in Atlantic City's so-called "wiener war," where the front line was drawn along the venerable boardwalk. Competing peddlers in the city's $6 million-a-year hot dog business bruised heads, bloodied noses and overturned each others' carts in violent confrontations at some of the lucrative vending spots in front of the casinos.

State police undercover agents posed as vendors to investigate. The outcome was the indictment of a dozen men identified with an effort by an allegedly mob-connected company called Island Vets, to take over Hot Digity Dogs, Inc., one of the few local business ventures still prospering. Among those named in the indictment was Edward Casale of Margate, New Jersey, identified by state police as an alleged enforcer for "Little Nicky" Scarfo, reputed boss of the Philadelphia-Atlantic City organized crime family.

The mobsters had been extorting up to $5,000 a week from Hot Digity Dogs. When legitimate vendors resisted, they got their heads cracked to remind them who the real bosses were.

"Keep Your Filthy Hands out of Atlantic City"

The incident was an ironic reminder of the day in 1976 when then Governor of New Jersey Brendan T. Byrne stood on the Atlantic City boardwalk and defiantly declared, "Organized crime is not welcome. I warn them, keep your filthy hands out of Atlantic City."[3] The casino

132

law he signed and celebrated that day was called the toughest in the world. The gambling industry in New Jersey is policed by 100 federal law enforcement agents, 126 state police and 750 state lawyers, accountants and inspectors. But, though unwelcome and threatened, the mob has managed serious inroads into the controversial new Atlantic City industry, lured by the enormous profits it generates.

"The state government can't control a huge cash industry like this," said New Jersey's Democratic Congressman, Robert G. Torricelli. "It's like saying Seattle can control Boeing. The industry ends up controlling the state. We were naive to think we could keep out organized crime," he acknowledges. "Now we recognize that the price of legalized gambling is that we become the focus of attention for undesirable elements."[4]

Raiding the Slot Machines

Between 1978 and 1983, those undesirables stole from Nevada casinos alone an estimated $80 million, according to James Avance, Chairman of the Nevada Gaming Control Board. What annoys the gaming control people is that during those four key years the state was cheated out of more than $4.6 million it would have collected in taxes on those additional profits. The IRS lost a similar sum.

Nevada's 400 casinos operate more than 90,000 slot machines, and there is no way to tell how many of these were ripped off—or still are being outwitted. "It could have involved much more than the $20 million per year we have estimated," Avance says. "No one really knows."[5]

This particular skullduggery came to light quite accidently on the afternoon of August 19, 1983, when a casino patron named Constantine G. Econopoulos hit a $1.7 million jackpot on the progressive dollar slot machines at Harrah's Hotel and Casino in Lake Tahoe. The happy Greek became an instant celebrity, and his picture—standing next to the winning machine—was a highlight of that evening's TV news in the San Francisco Bay area where he lived. He held in his hand the first installment on his killing: a Harrah's check for $200,000.

The Police Also Were Tuned In

Unfortunately for Econopoulos, however, the San Francisco police were watching TV that evening, and an alert detective recognized the instant millionaire as a convicted felon who had been the guest of the state on two occasions over a 12-year period on burglary raps.

Meanwhile, Harrah's had installed Econopoulos in a luxurious suite as its guest while Nevada agents began a routine check of the slot machine that had provided his bonanza. This particular check, however, proved very *un*routine. The agents found that the supposedly tamper-proof machine and its encased microchip computer heart had been meddled with.

Harrah's promptly stopped payment on the check and the no-longer-overjoyed Greek was taken into custody. It took a while, but in due time the pieces fell into place. Members of his gang had stood casually around the machine to block casino surveillance cameras while a "mechanic" opened and reset the machine, programming it to give up the jackpot under conditions they controlled. Econopoulos was merely the "claimer" who stepped forward to collect the jackpot—a performance for which he was promised 20 percent of the action. Now casinos are pondering how many millions other entrepeneurs have diverted from their cash flow without the losses being discovered.

Declining Profits in the Industry

The fact is, with profits declining, 10 percent of Nevada's casinos have gone bankrupt in recent years. The competition is awesome. Las Vegas has more than 50 casinos and some 50,000 hotel rooms—not to mention another 350 or so gambling centers in other parts of Nevada. "We no longer have a monopoly," observes Las Vegas banker E. Parry Thomas. The threat comes largely from Atlantic City. "Atlantic City has one thing we'll never have," Thomas points out. "That is 60 million people only half a gasoline tank away."[6]

Comparatively few Atlantic City casinos end up dividing the business—with only 15 casinos and 9,000 rooms. Yet even that advantage is no guarantee of success. Already one Atlantic City casino is bankrupt and others are loudly singing the blues.

No doubt more of them will go under—particularly in view of the determined efforts of Miami Beach hotel owners to provide even more competition through a county-option legalizing of casinos in Florida. And that isn't likely to stifle other initiatives in New Orleans, Detroit, West Virginia, Ohio and elsewhere. For as long as people are willing to cough up their money in the cause of fun and excitement over the cards, the dice or the roulette wheel, accommodating wealthy investors

135

always will be there—happy to become even richer through gamblers' losses.

Opportunities Unlimited for Illegal Profits

We dare not overlook the significance of casinos in society's frenzied rush toward permissiveness. For many Americans, "casinos" are a synonym for gambling. If there is none within a couple of hours of where you live, be patient—someone probably will remedy that soon enough. Along with lotteries, casinos are the frothy edge of the wave that is washing the gambling craze across our nation.

Yet casinos differ significantly from lotteries in that the toll they take is far more cruel, and their earnings go primarily to private owners. Lottery profits—however questionable the ethics of the trend—at least benefit some citizens of their sponsoring states. Gambling casinos, on the other hand, channel most of their earnings to already wealthy entrepeneur owners and managers while offering to unscrupulous people in all walks of life almost unlimited opportunity for illegal profiteering.

Points to Ponder

---

1. Have you ever taken time to think about the urge of humans to gamble? Place most of us in front of a slot machine, and we experience that inexplicable urge to deposit a quarter and pull the handle—even though we know the probability of losing exceeds the possi-

136

bility of winning. Suppose, in no more than three short sentences, you were required to explain why that impulse grips us. What would you write?

2. In a five-way slot machine, winning symbols can line up in one of three rows straight across or in either of two angled rows like a big X, with each way costing an additional quarter. The sales pitch is that this "increases your chance of winning." Does betting five times as much with five times as many chances of winning really make us more likely to win?

3. Would a gambling casino be described best as "a place where people win a lot of money" or "a place where people lose a lot of money"? Where do casinos get the money an occasional winner walks away with? Do they print it, import it from outer space or perhaps dig it up on the beach?

4. Do the people who own casinos know they will always come out ahead, or is there a sense in which they "gamble" like their customers?

5. Don't answer without giving it some serious thought, but, as a Christian, what does money symbolize to you? If you have a $10- or a $20-bill—even a $5—bill will do, hold it in your hand for a while and reflect on what that piece of paper means. Is it really yours, or do you hold it in joint ownership with someone else? What about your husband or wife, your child or parent, your bank or mortgage company or—dare we suggest it—God?

Notes

1. From a personal 2 A.M. interview with the author at Paradise Island Casino, Bahamas.
2. Ibid.
3. *Washington Post,* January 16, 1984.
4. Ibid.
5. *Chicago Tribune,* September 19, 1984, sect. 1, p. 4.
6. *U.S. News & World Report,* May 30, 1983.

10

Loopholes and High Rollers

Bᴜᴛ ᴜɴᴅᴇʀᴡᴏʀʟᴅ ATTRACTION and profiteering are not the only threats to our well-being that link themselves with gambling casinos. They also serve as clearing houses for money that would cause serious embarrassment if someone traced it to its sources.

Casinos are not just glitzy palaces where hysterically happy citizens may gamble away their savings, incur ruinous debts and have themselves a ball in the process. They also can provide enticing tax advantages for those wily enough to claim them and a no-questions-asked laundering facility for "dirty" money generated in both legitimate and illigitimate business enterprises.

Illicit Use of the Cash Transaction

In "legitimate" business, the cash transaction is a widely used method of siphoning off unlawful profits, avoiding tax liability, concealing involvement by disreputable characters and masking the details of hidden ownership. The basis for the cash transaction can be just about anything—a piece of real estate, ownership in a business, heirloom jewelry, a truckload of hijacked TV sets or some type of questionable professional service. For some complicated reason the item goes for half its real value—at least on the books. The balance is paid in cash as "shoe box money."

What makes the deal potentially profitable to all concerned is that no one is accountable for the balance. No one can prove it; no one need know about it. The money appears on no one's books, and thus may slip through the cracks of sales tax, document tax or income tax liability—plus the advantage of leaving an unfathomable uncertainty about who did what for whom and how much he got for the favor.

Sooner or later, however, soaring cash money must come down to earth and appear in someone's records—and that's where casinos step in. No matter how clandestine the business transaction, in due time someone will need to know where the money went or how the owner got it—someone curious and inquisitive like, say, company auditors, agents of the Federal Bureau of Investigation or people who work for the Internal Revenue Service. This is true for the person who forks over the cash—who may have to explain to someone what happened to it—as well as for the person who pockets the cash and has to have a plausible story about the source from which it came. To have won it or lost it at the casino is an explanation no one can disprove.

A Fistful of $100 or $1000 Bills

The seller may have a fistful of attention-getting $100 or $1000 bills, but no feasible way to get them

140

back into the legitimate monetary mainstream. Paying income taxes on the money may not, in fact, be his problem. He might be willing to pay the taxes if only he could conceal the episode from other prying eyes. Bank deposits—particularly large ones—can come under embarrassingly close scrutiny by state and federal boards or commissions concerned with the legitimacy of financial transactions.

This dilemma can be all the more crucial for the drug dealer, racketeer or extortioner who may make a modest salary at a cover-up job but takes in considerably more than that from his illicit activities. He urgently needs a laundering facility where he can provide a proper ancestry for cash of spurious origin.

What more convenient solution to this dilemma than the gambling casino? There, millions of dollars in cash and checks change hands nightly with no questions asked and no answers necessary. From whatever source they may come, illegal dollars can be legitimized through a process that provides a deliberately casual *un*accountability—with the carefree delights of the gambling tables thrown in at no extra charge.

The seller brings his cash to the casino where he may already have earned acceptance as a high roller. There he may, of course, lose it all—in which case the question of tax liability is conveniently resolved. But he probably knows better than to let that happen. He may win or lose a little, depending on his skill or good luck or lack of it, and then he will go his way—the happy possessor of a stack of $1000 bills or, better yet, a check or draft, allegedly won at dice, cards or roulette. No one can prove he *didn't* win it there. Now he has a credible source for that tidy sum which, until he arrived at the

141

casino, had considerable potential for embarrassment, if not outright culpability.

The Skim, the Kickback and the Bribe

Cash transactions, of course, are not the only sources of "dirty" money in business—though they may be the most commonplace. There is also the skim, the kickback and the business bribe, and there is the reality of cash from outright theft—very hot cash, burning the proverbial hole in the culprit's pocket.

Skimming is a simple term that describes the act of siphoning off into someone's pockets a portion of the money that forms the life's blood of a business enterprise. Owners and managers may have the most enticing opportunities to skim, but they aren't the only culprits. Cash can be misappropriated in the business arena by anyone from owners and managers right down through the hierarchy to the lowest paid employee on the payroll. At that lower level, however, it is usually referred to as theft—an act of betrayal considered somewhat less honorable than skimming at the top. No matter how elaborate the precautionary measures, dishonest people in the world of commerce still manage here and there to dip into the cash and get away with it. Some may never be caught.

Every retail business that accepts cash for goods or services—from the largest department store chain down to the smallest local shop—offers an open invitation to skimming or theft and, presumably, as long as humans remain human, the skimmers and thieves will continue to stalk their prey. But auditing agencies are making it increasingly difficult for people to account for large sums of money fraudulently acquired. That is why gambling casinos can provide a welcome relief for the frustrations unique to skimmers and corporate thieves.

Vast Amounts of Dirty Money in Circulation

Vast amounts of dirty money circulate constantly in these United States. Whatever can lend an air of legitimacy to illegally obtained cash and neutralize the embarrassment of identifying its source provides a valuable helping hand to those who conduct their financial affairs, of necessity, in the shadows. Finding it buried under a rock isn't a very convincing story. Casinos provide a solution to that dilemma.

Knowledgeable people in the gaming business may not advertise the fact, but they are well aware that "good players" tend to be people from businesses or professions in the higher echelons of cash flow. Most high rollers come to the casino from businesses likely to generate unaccountable cash—money derived from large, untraceable and untaxed transactions. When the cash comes in large sums, it may need to be laundered. Casinos are delighted to provide the washing machine.

$37.3 Million in Pampering Services

During 1983, Chairman Stephen A. Wynn posted profits of $35.9 million for his Golden Nugget in Atlantic City—nearly doubling what the casino had earned two years before. He accomplished that feat primarily by *more* than doubling his giveaway budget to attract high rollers to the Golden Nugget—posting $37.3 million in pampering services. Casino analysts speculate that

143

Chairman Wynn stands guard over a list of approximately 600 adventurous and affluent players who account for at least 60 percent of his table business. He treats those special players like kings and queens, and they pay him royally for the privilege. Would anyone suppose the Golden Nugget screens those special guests to be sure the money is clean? Would someone suggest anyone cares?

Sands Hotel and Casino president William Weidner is credited with the most lavish giveaway seduction of high rollers. He is credited with presenting a $56,000 Mercedes to one of his favored customers. On another occasion he bought seats on the luxurious supersonic Concorde to spirit 40 of his high-rolling friends and their wives off on a junket to Monte Carlo.

In spite of all that, however, his profits lagged behind those of Golden Nugget, Caesar's Palace and Resorts International, so Weidner began a program he calls "matching 'em and upping 'em one." In the fall of 1984 he opened seven "wildman suites" designed to attract the attention of high rollers like the Connecticut businessman reputed to have lost nearly $1 million at the Sands during that same year. Losers like that may choose between transportation from home or office to Atlantic City on the casino's $3.2 million Sikorsky S-76 helicopter or from their local airports aboard an equally expensive Mitsubishi Diamond Jet.

Those Dazzling High-Roller Suites

When the high roller checks in at the Sands, he will likely be housed amid the dazzling mirrors and polished Italian marble of the Versailles Suite. Five-foot portraits

144

of Louis XVI and Marie Antoinette adorn the silken walls and add design authenticity to the modern Jacuzzi, spacious sauna, pool table and environmental tank.

Back at the Golden Nugget, well-heeled guests can enjoy worth-their-weight-in-gold antiques, grand pianos and original paintings by the masters. One suite boasts an oriental alcove housing a six-foot Buddha. For those eager for every possible advantage before entering the gambling arena, a place is provided for a brief act of worship in front of the Gautama's rotund figure. Serious gamblers, we presume, are careful to touch all the bases.

But all of these good things depend, of course, on what the computer shows concerning the high roller's losses at the gaming tables. Even in Las Vegas and Atlantic City, there is no free lunch. As long as the jet or helicopter leaves him off at home considerably less affluent than when it picked him up, the hospitality of the host casino knows no bounds. Neither is it likely to ask him where all the easy money came from.

Untraceable, Untaxed Money in Abundance

Untraceable and untaxed money apparently exists in abundance today. Harvard University's James Henry observed in 1976 that the very nature of paper currency available in this country suggests a wide evasion or defiance of accountability requirements. The United States boasts $80 to $85 billion in currency, and approximately 25 percent of that is in $1 to $10 bills. Another 35 percent is in $50 and $100 bills. The remaining 40 percent is in even larger denominations.

Most of us, in everyday transactions, avoid carrying

145

bills larger than the ubiquitous $20, though a single $20 bill seldom gets us past the supermarket checkout counter any more. In fact, many businesses are suspicious of a $20 bill and definitely frown on a $50 bill. Almost none will accept a $100 bill without the closest possible scrutiny and a probing identification check.

Banks traditionally hold as little cash as they can get by with in adequately serving their depositors' needs—reportedly only about 20 percent of the currency in existence in this country. As a matter of policy, they stock very little in the way of large bills. Banks carry less than 5 percent of paper denominations larger than the $50 bill. One reason, of course, is that there is very little demand for the big ones—at least in legitimate areas of financial transaction. Another reason is that cash money in a bank vault or a teller's drawer is earning no interest for the bank.

Drug Dealers Hold $20 Billion in Currency

What all of that means is that, once the currency held by banks and legitimate users is accounted for, something in excess of $30 billion remains in hands unknown. This is mostly in larger bills, and it is reasonable to assume the bills are held substantially by people engaged in businesses or professions functioning only through large, untraceable, noncredit transactions carried on behind the scenes or under the table. At any given moment, principals in the illicit drug business alone across our nation may be holding as much as $20 billion in currency of large denominations!

Casinos provide probably the largest and most reliable facilities for laundering dirty money questionably acquired. That laundering requires no illicit activity on the part of the casinos and no collusion between management and the player. Everything is legal, and no one is liable. Money is money—however spotless or stained its origin.

The people who operate America's casinos have no obligation to question the character of players who step up to the cashier's window or to the dice, blackjack or roulette tables and lay cash on the line. Nor are they concerned about the scruples or the reputations of the high rollers to whom they provide free junkets with lavish complimentary accommodations. The source of the money wagered or traded for chips is not their concern.

What casinos are all about is action at the tables with a percentage to the house—and the larger the amounts wagered the fatter the percentage. The money is the medium, and the medium is indeed the message. Money is the common denominator that reduces to a single level the drug dealer, the bookmaker, the petty thief, the loan shark, the arsonist, the skimmer, the tax evader and the legitimate businessman seeking harmless enjoyment at the gaming tables. It is no secret that a few professing Christians can also be found at the heart of that mixed multitude.

A World of Unquestioning Acceptance

In that frame of reference, the casino provides a characteristically undiscriminating environment for its clientele. Here is a setting in which acceptance of the player is based not on wealth, beauty, achievement, skill or family name, but on the size and frequency of the bet and the ability to pay off losses. Casinos can claim to be

147

among the most democratic of our institutions.

In the world outside, the player may be a dentist or a drug dealer, a race driver or a racketeer, a minister or a mobster, a physician or a pimp, but within the casino's four walls he finds a world of unquestioning acceptance. He may even attract a bit of long coveted admiration or a fleeting glimpse of fame if he scores a spectacular win. In fact, at the gaming tables a special kind of admiration may even be meted out to the spectacular *loser* if he handles his losses like a seasoned professional.

The casino can be whatever the player needs it to be. If that is to be a clearing house for tainted cash, that poses no problem for the management—as long as the house gets its cut.

The Desire for Recognition

And why do otherwise intelligent, discreet, perceptive and successful tycoons persist in the obvious sham of the high-roller game? Psychologists theorize, if it isn't just to clean up tainted money, it probably is because of that insatiable human desire for recognition. All humans share to some extent the need to be perceived as somebody special—even though we may be reasonably sure that in reality we are not.

The words "brash" and "cocky" often appear when observers attempt verbal descriptions of high rollers. Now and then the favored customers are simply compulsive gamblers who have enough money from some source or another to support their expensive habit, and who bask in the special attention earned by their sometimes shocking losses.

148

Keeping Them Betting,
Losing and Betting Again

"Where do you see this high-roller program taking the industry in the future?" one casino executive was asked when he grumbled over the alleged $2,000 an hour it costs to operate his special delivery helicopter.

"Just about anywhere it wants to lead us," he replied, a bit whimsically. "Some of our best people lie awake at night just thinking up new things to give away—ways to excite our regular customers to keep them from losing interest. We don't think of it in terms of extravagance or waste—just in terms of how much we get in return when they hit those casino tables.

"It's spending money to make money," he said. "We run a business here like any other enterprise, and whatever we can give them—as long as it's legal—that will keep them betting and losing and coming back to bet and lose again, we'll sure be handing it over, no matter how ridiculous it seems to somebody out there or how much it costs us to give it away."[1]

Is That Your Value System?

Is this, then, the value system with which the conscientious Christian wishes to be identified? Emphatically not, when he is instructed to "beware lest ye also, being led away with the error of the wicked, fall from your own steadfastness. But grow in grace, and in the knowledge of our Lord and Saviour Jesus Christ" (2 Pet. 3:17,18). He isn't doing much growing in that urgently important knowledge while rubbing shoulders with greed at the slot machines, the craps table or the roulette wheel.

149

But, then, maybe he never got a good, clear look before at the world of loopholes and high rollers. Maybe he thought laundering had to do only with dirty clothes, not with dirty money!

Points to Ponder

1. Why is it important that people who deal in illicit transactions pay or be paid in cash? Is it only to avoid income tax liability or are there other complications making it necessary that no records be kept? How can gambling casinos or bookies provide a solution for their problems?
2. The skim, the kickback and the bribe are three potential sources of fraudulent profit in the business arena. If a Christian has evidence that someone in his company is skimming cash before it is accounted for, accepting a kickback from someone in return for purchasing his goods or services, or being bribed because someone has something on him, do you feel that Christian has a moral responsibility to do something about it? What, for example?
3. You may not see this as a serious possibility, but suppose you had obtained, say, $100,000 in a fraudulent transaction. How would you go about explaining your sudden prosperity to (a) your spouse, (b) your children, (c) your closest friend, (d) the people at church?
4. If someone provided you with free helicopter transportation from your home to his gambling casino,

plus a complimentary luxury hotel suite with gourmet meals as long as you stayed there, would you suspect ulterior motives or would you consider him just a nice, eccentric rich friend who loves to make you happy?

5. Do people who operate casinos have an obligation to ask players at the cashier's window where their money comes from? Should they require character references on everyone who bets more than, say, $1,000 at a time? If not, how do you think gambling casinos could lessen the possibility of being used by unscrupulous people to launder larger sums of dirty money?

Note
1. *Wall Street Journal,* December 27, 1984.

11

Managing the Point Spread

WITH CASINOS BEHIND US, adding texture to the nation's gambling picture takes us to America's favorite—and most costly—indulgence: betting on the outcome of sports events. Whether through friendly "betcha 10 bucks" wagers, office sports pools or full-fledged bookie operations—sports betting far outdistances casinos, lotteries and even bingo in terms of gambling dollars changing hands. Americans appear obsessed with the idea of predicting winners in games and races. "Which team beats which team or which horse beats which horse is what our business is all about," a bookmaker described his profession.

He Believes He Helps His Team Win

Sports enthusiasts develop remarkable loyalty for their favorite teams. Psychologists say this loyalty can result in the perception that when a fan bets on his team he is actually helping it to win. He is demonstrating his loyalty in a tangible way he feels may even intimidate the opposition. His bet is an effective challenge to those who do not share his faith in his team, and the more reckless his wager the more intimidating to them is his gesture of loyalty. "Put your money where your mouth is!" and "Put up or shut up!" have silenced many sports enthusiasts less confident of their cause. There is no clinical evidence, however, that such loyalty ever has turned a loser into a winner.

Predictably, the sports activities that get the most press notice also get the most action from betting enthusiasts. Before a new team franchise has earned widespread name recognition, it will inspire only minimal action in the betting arena. Even then, it takes major seasonal sports—at professional college levels—to attract the big betting bucks. "Football or baseball, basketball and hockey are my bread and butter," a big-city bookie acknowledged. "They give us a year-round schedule to work with, and we like steady income as well as the next guy. Before one seasonal sport shuts down, another has started up, and that means there's very little break in the action—or the income."

The Surest and Easiest Way to Turn a Fast Buck

But uninterrupted action and steady income are not the only benefits the bookmaker derives from betting based on the outcome of major sports events. The potential for greater profits in sports betting also is what motivates him to specialize. He theorizes that, for whatever reasons, sports enthusiasts have more money to bet than those who prefer other types of gambling. Bookies aren't overly concerned about why that phenomenon exists; they just see sports wagering as a gaming indulgence patronized more by the affluent than by nickle-and-dime gamblers, and that means greater return on the time and effort they invest in soliciting and processing the bets. After all, they're in the business not because they are sportsmen but because for them this is the surest and easiest way to turn a fast buck.

In spite of his illicit profession, the bookmaker often commands a certain professional respect among his clients. They wouldn't invite him over for dinner or be seen with him at a charity ball, but they tend to regard him as a broker of sorts. He brings together money on both sides of an athletic contest, and he probably feels a fiduciary responsibility to his clients. If he hopes to stay in business, however, he must arrange it so that the money pumped in by his losers will more than cover the money he pays out to his winners. That means he must skillfully manipulate the figures to keep the betting odds in his favor.

Managing to keep that odds-on advantage is, in fact, the most significant challenge of his trade. Those odds must not be great enough to discourage his customers from putting money on the line and dreaming of the big win, yet they must be tilted sufficiently in the bookie's favor to guarantee a generous return on his investment. The bookie can't afford to gamble; his income must be a sure thing.

$10,000 Profit in a Good Week

Most sports bookmakers live well above the poverty level—and this fact is confirmed by the consistency of organized crime involvement in sports betting. The keys to big bucks for the bookie include (1) the affluence of sports wagerers as a class, (2) the skill of the bookmaker in "balancing" his wagers and (3) the regularity with which his choice customers risk large sums of money on the outcome of athletic events. Some well-established bookies would decline a bet of less than $100, and some boast regular clients who would not stoop to a wager of less than $5000.

The bookie's net income is likely to approach 5 percent of the gross amount wagered with him in both directions, even after runners, salesmen, clerks, telephone relayers, watchmen, collectors and other team members have been paid off. Enterprising bookies can net $10,000 in clear profit in a good week with properly managed point spreads, and it is doubtful that they tithe that income to support the work of the Lord.

It might be noted, in passing, that—since accounts payable as well as accounts receivable all are handled in cash transactions—bookmaking as a profession is not noted for its compliance with income tax laws.

The more his customers bet, the more money remains in the pockets of the bookmaker. The three sources from which he generates that income are (1) the point spread or handicap, (2) the "vigorish"[1] surrendered by the losers and (3) the tips he can count on receiving from grateful winners.

Determining the Point Spread

Handicapping, for the bookie, is a relatively simple process, accomplished primarily by applying to win/lose wagers the point spread—however speculative—established by recognized experts in the sports field.

Jimmy "the Greek" Snyder probably is the best known among those entrepeneurs, though others like the Churchill Downs Sports Book in Las Vegas and J.K. Sports with several offices in California also help dictate what is known as the "line" or the "spot" for sports betting. In spite of the fact that bookmaking is illegal, these point spreads are published in the sports sections of hundreds of newspapers across the country. Since they are quoted always in whole points, however—as, for example, the Redskins are favored over the Jets by 14 points—the published point spreads are classified as "nonwagering" lines. Thus newspapers that print them remain unchallenged by officials charged with enforcing antigambling laws.

What makes whole point spreads impractical where wagering is involved is that if Washington at $+14$ beats New York by exactly two touchdowns, the result is the same as a tie or "push." All bets are off. And ties offer neither excitement for the gambler nor profit for the bookie. If the score is tied when the handicap is factored in, no money changes hands—and money, not team competition, is the real name of the game.

Point spreads represent the experts' calculation of the theoretical difference in strength between opposing teams. These point spreads are based on detailed comparisons of past team or individual performances, and on any special circumstances that might influence the outcome of the game—like an injured star unable to start, a pass receiver caught in a distracting marital conflict or a quarterback known to be struggling with a pass release problem. The element of chance still is there, however, and the experts have been known to be spectacularly wrong in their posting of the odds.

In some cases the circumstances of a team or of a contest are considered so unpredictable that the game is declared "off the board," with no wagers accepted on either side. An "in the circle" classification warns that wagers are accepted at a calculated risk. In other cases, bookmakers may accept bets on certain games only with definite stipulations—for example, it's all off if Bronco Sullivan doesn't start at nose guard.

Making Money Is the Bookie's Goal

The most important criterion for a wagering line is, of course, that it make money for the bookie. To accomplish this, it must attract balanced amounts of betting money on each side in the contest and assure a payoff, whatever the final score. With that purpose in mind, the bookie works from, say, Jimmy the Greek's line of two touchdowns but hikes up his own odds on the Redskins to $14\frac{1}{2}$ points. That means that a bet placed on the underdog Jets gets the benefit of being spotted $14\frac{1}{2}$ points, and a bet on the favored Redskins gives up the same number of points. There is no way a team can score that extra one-half point, so there can be no ties.

Customers who bet on Washington are *losers* if it outscores New York by only two touchdowns. Anyone who bet on the Redskins is poorer by the amount of his wager—plus a 10 percent vigorish. That add-on percentage represents, in effect, the bookmaker's "brokerage fee." If the Washington rooter bet $5,000 and lost, he owes his bookie $5,000, plus the $500 vigorish. If he won, he doubtless expressed his gratitude with a generous tip.

One tricky problem with point spreads is that they

158

often are changed unexpectedly—and sometimes at the last minute. This means the bookie must keep a careful record of the exact amounts of all his bets with the precise point spread at the times the bets were taken. If he gets heavily committed at unfavorable spreads, he must offset that potential loss by at least an equal number of bets with a more favorable handicap. Or he must "lay off" the unbalanced side of the wager by placing balancing bets with other bookies. His daily routine is a constant juggling act, handling mathematical formulas of sometimes challenging complexity. In the end, the bookmakers divide among themselves the dollars sports wagerers funnel into their carefully organized cash flow system.

Juggling the Books

Bookmakers do sometimes pay off winners, by the way. Sports bettors win now and then—though not often enough, on the average, to keep them on the profit side of the ledger. That is why bookies must develop the ability to keep separate "balanced books" that determine how many wagers they will accept on each sporting event—and even from whom they will accept them.

If some of the bookie's customers bet a total of $40,000 on the Redskins at that $+14\frac{1}{2}$ point spread, and others bet only $23,000 on the Jets, he is in a vulnerable position he probably considers unacceptable. For one thing, that out-of-balance book means the general consensus among his street-smart customers is that the Redskins are going to win by more than two touchdowns. If the customers are right, he will have to pay off $40,000 while collecting only $23,000—plus, of course, the 10 percent vigorish charged the losers. That is not the way to stay solvent. He urgently needs more bets on the New York team.

The bookmaker accomplishes this by increasing the point spread for all new bets to, say, 17½. That means wagers on New York made after that increase will pay off even if Washington leads by two touchdowns plus an extra point at the closing whistle. Now more of his clients will get interested in backing New York with "a dollar" ($100), "a nickel" ($500) or even "a dime" ($1,000). His new odds encourage more Jets bets, and the assets and liabilities that hinge on that particular contest move back in the direction of an acceptable balance.

Obviously the bookie who develops a few reliable mathematical formulas and a keen sensitivity to favorable point spreads is far more likely to succeed in this shady business than the one who depends on chance or instinct alone. He can count on his vigorish, and he will get those gratuities from grateful winners, but if he allows his book to get badly out of balance on the side of an inadequate point spread he may find himself in serious financial difficulty. A couple of sizeable losses could catapult him—however unwillingly—into some less risky profession with the impossible requirement of regular office hours. That unique occupational hazard called "point spread," is why the turnover in bookies tends to be more rapid than in more stable lines of work.

Underworld Backing Balances the Books

Our nation is generously populated, however, with well-established bookmakers whose financial resources are sufficient to let them ride out the occasional risk of unbalanced books. Thanks to that vigorish, to the customary gratuities, to underworld backing and to their professional know-how, the odds are solidly on their side in the long run. Veteran bookies can analyze point spreads and manipulate betting odds in their favor, and they understand much better than their clients the workings of the law of averages.

Because the big bucks of organized crime are behind most big-time bookies, a strict balance in the bets they book on any single event is not as crucial to their survival as it might be in the case of a less adequately subsidized competitor. These big-timers are the bookies who remain on the job year in and year out. They develop expanding lists of trusting and trusted followers who place with them bets totaling hundreds of thousands of dollars each week. They also generate incredibly large sums of money for controlling mob figures.

Anonymity Is a Necessity

Most of bookie transactions are handled by telephone. Wins and losses are paid off later, usually through runners or collectors. Bookmakers maintain as much distance as possible from their clients. They take on new customers slowly and cautiously. They keep records that, of necessity, are coded, vague, anonymous and ambiguous.

Bookies live and function in a world of almost exaggerated secrecy—and for good reasons. They live in constant danger of detection and apprehension. They know that people charged with enforcing the laws—unless paid to look the other way—are eager to penetrate into their inner circle and gather evidence to convict them of law violation. They also know that their betting customers live in potentially explosive emotional environments.

Losers' attitudes can be dramatically different from those of winners. A winning client who is enthusiastic about the bookmaking operation today could become a disgruntled loser tomorrow—and therefore a threat. A drastic change of heart for whatever reasons could tempt even a once-loyal friend to turn state's evidence and lower the boom on the illicit bookmaking operation.

Bookies Are Hard to Catch

Yet, the truth is, law enforcement officers consider bookies singularly difficult to apprehend and prosecute. The industry is prosperous enough to provide a generous unaudited cash reserve out of which protection money can be designated for corruptible members of the enforcement community. The backing of organized crime ensures swift bond-out and delayed prosecution if an arrest does happen to be made. The paraphernalia the bookmaking industry uses, combined with the process by which it functions, is designed to drag a host of "herrings" across the trail for any crusader setting out to break up an illicit operation.

Take "Backstraps," for example. These are ubiquitous devices that enable bookies to move their telephones to new locations without the knowledge of the telephone company. "Cheeseboxes" are installed between two telephone lines so the customer's call on the number given him is automatically transferred to another number only the bookmaker knows. Some bookmakers employ answering services—anonymously or under fictitious names—which they query periodically to collect the coded names or numbers of betting customers they are to call. Recording devices are popular—especially those that can be queried anonymously with a coded *beeper* from another telephone to pick up the names or numbers of clients who want to place a bet.

Automatic call-forwarding services provided by telephone companies have proven professionally helpful to thousands of bookies. Through this relatively inexpensive service they can provide customers with a number to call, yet maintain secrecy concerning the number or the location of the telephone where the bet actually is placed.

The Elderly and Tradesmen Are Made Accessories

Some bookmakers employ third parties—frequently elderly individuals with no criminal records who need a little income to stretch their Social Security stipend—to take the names and numbers of wagerers who call. Periodically, from a location known only to himself, the bookmaker checks in to pick up the names or numbers.

The function of the bookmaking system usually depends upon a network of people at various levels who bring together the client and the bookie, generate and pass along information about point spreads and wagers and then transport often large sums of money between losers and winners. The best sources of such "middleman" help are the trades with ready access to the public—people like bartenders, waitresses, taxi drivers, doormen, parking valets and newspaper vendors.

Of equal importance to the system are the loan sharks and the enforcers who are called into action when collection problems arise. The interest charged by the shylocks may be blatantly usurous—1 percent a day, 5 percent a week or sometimes more. Where the operation involves organized crime, the interest—and this, too, is referred to as "vigorish"—can *double* each month that the amount is owed. Not to pay as promised is to risk missing teeth, a broken leg or a threat against the safety of loved ones. In "hopeless" collection cases, a gang-style execution might set an example for others tempted to deal irresponsibly with those offbeat lending institutions.

Dangerous to Your Health

Bookmakers often are considered knowledgeable professionals, trusted confidants and understanding friends, but clients do well not to forget that the primary interest of bookies is easy money—with as few scruples involved as possible. They have been known to undergo swift and unexpected character changes. The operators who make book can become both dangerous to health and a threat to longevity when clients forget that they are in it for the big bucks.

The *Achilles' heel* most common to bookies is the necessity to keep careful accounts of all their wagers. Without these accounts the system could not function; yet with them the bookmaker is vulnerable to detection by the vice squad. These records can become convincing evidence for judges and juries when arrests have been made and alleged violators of criminal codes brought to trial.

Elaborate coded systems of recording wagers, point spreads, accounts payable and accounts receivable, therefore, are among the professional accoutrements of a successful bookie. These records must tell him all he needs to know to keep his affairs in order, yet not reveal to a possible arresting officer, an FBI agent or the IRS what can be used to convict him on illegal bookmaking or income tax evasion charges. It is especially important that his records not reveal the identity of his customers. They could be charged with misdemeanors themselves; that would prove very bad indeed for them—and for business.

So be warned: Doing business with a bookie can damage your health and reputation; it is even more likely to injure your bank account, and it most certainly will not enhance your walk with the Lord.

Points to Ponder

1. Psychologists say some wagerers actually feel they are helping their team win when they place a bet. The more reckless the wager, the greater the loyalty and the more intimidating the gesture—or so it is thought. Have you ever felt you should defend the reputation of your favorite team when someone offered to bet against it? Was that the reason you bet?
2. "Put your money where your mouth is" is a time-worn challenge for someone to bet money instead of

bragging or making claims. Why do you think humans feel so strongly the need to relate their being right—or superior—with the winning or losing of money?

3. What does "point spread" mean in the bookie's vocabulary? Who decides by how many points the Dolphins, say, are supposed to win over the Patriots? Why is it important to bookies that the spread be quoted in terms of ½ a point?

4. Why must a bookie keep what he calls "balanced books"? If he finds himself vulnerable to a possibly costly loss, what are the two strategies he can use to get back in balance again? Do these strategies affect the chances to win of those who already have placed bets with him?

5. Suppose you were a law enforcement officer attempting to get evidence on someone you believed was engaged in bookmaking. How would you penetrate the curtain of secrecy that shrouds his operation? How would you persuade the people you felt would be effective witnesses to testify against him?

Note

1. "Vigorish" is probably of Yiddish origin, in turn coming from the Russian word *vyigrysh* meaning "winnings" or "profit." In the language of the betting world, vigorish is the charge made on bets by, say, a bookie or a gambling house. The term can also refer to the interest a borrower pays a moneylender. *Webster's Ninth New Dictionary* (New York: Merriam-Webster Inc., Publishers, 1985), p. 1315.

12
The Elusive Alfie Mart

ALFIE MART STAYED out of jail for more than 30 years, in spite of the fact that he managed a wide-open bookmaking operation on Miami Beach which probably netted him up to $5 million a year.

Finally, in 1975, the state's attorney succeeded in locking him up briefly in Dade County's correctional facility. That happened, however, only because of a series of chance circumstances. A Beach cop who recognized him when he slipped into a telephone booth on Lincoln Road sneaked up to eavesdrop on the conversation. He heard talk of odds and point spreads, and he made an arrest based on probable cause. Alfie was carrying unmistakable gambling paraphernalia, and that is a misdemeanor under Florida law. The four-month imprisonment the county judge handed him was Alfie's first incarceration.

A Liberal Policy Toward Gamblers

Once upon a time almost everyone in Miami Beach knew Alfie and how he made his living. He was the city's oldest and least touchable bookmaker. "He's sort of grandfathered in," commented a retired city commissioner who knew all about Alfie and his illegal profession back in the late '40s. It seems not many people in those days were interested in spoiling the fun. Politicians convinced Miami Beach voters the fickle, wealthy visitors in town made necessary a "liberal policy" toward the enforcement of gambling laws. They said it was necessary to the survival of the tourist trade. No one doubted that some of the politicians were paid well for their liberality.

Since gambling was considered good for the economy, it followed that people like Alfie who provided the means of gambling were as respectable as those who looked the other way when the bookmaker plied his trade.

Alfie the bookmaker still, in fact, is considered a prominent man in his natural habitat. He is a longtime member of the Miami Beach Optimists Club and is credited with the founding of his civic group's youth baseball league. The Optimists Club has awarded him a plaque of honor for his service to the community. He is carried on synagogue rolls at the fashionable Temple Beth Sholom. His son, Skip, was a star quarterback on the Miami Beach High School football team two decades ago. In the spirit of *mitzvah*—Yiddish for doing good deeds without seeking recognition—Alfie has made a specialty of hiring as night porters some of the Beach's chronic alcoholics to give them a little boost along the road to sobriety. The evidence indicates that he had the means with which to do it.

"Great guy," former Beach Mayor Harold Rosen commented to a *Miami Herald* reporter doing a follow-up story. "Nice fellow," ventured Rocky Pomerance, once the local police chief and formerly president of the International Association of Chiefs of Police.[1]

"A Local Boy Who's Never Hurt Anybody"

Alfie agrees with that assessment. "I've never done anything wrong," he insists. "I'm just a local boy, and I've never done anything to hurt anybody." And how does he feel about the cops who now seek to shut down his operation? "They should be out catching criminals," grunts Alfie.[2]

Through the years, of course, there were a few inevitable brushes with the law. But these proved nothing to cause a well-established bookie anything more than minor inconvenience.

The Miami Beach police records show Alfie first was arrested on a charge of illegal bookmaking in 1950, but for reasons not recorded the charges were not pressed. He was represented in this little "misunderstanding" by an attorney retained by the old S. & G. Syndicate, a local organization operating under a Florida state corporate charter out of a swank penthouse suite on Lincoln Road. The Syndicate was suspected of controlling all Miami Beach vice—which was plenty.

In those days, people with money enough could buy anything they wanted on the Beach, legal or not. Bookies set up shop in hotel lobbies on corner settees. Prostitutes worked from barstools in most of the popular lounges. Smoke-filled back rooms on the South End provided the dice and card tables many winter visitors were seeking.

S. & G. Syndicate members, according to Alfie, were

really just local boys—a feature far more desirable, he insists, than allowing "mobsters from New York and Chicago" to control the action. "No Mafia members were allowed," says Alfie as he reminisces on those golden days. "If you had an Italian name or a mustache, you'd soon find yourself on the outside."[3]

Up Front, a Legitimate Businessman

The year 1950 also was the time Tennessee Senator Estes Kefauver organized his Special Committee to Investigate Organized Crime in Interstate Commerce, which accumulated substantial evidence of close ties between gambling syndicates and local political officials—Miami Beach included. The presence of Kefauver Committee members in South Florida apparently cooled Syndicate operations temporarily, and Alfie decided to become, at least up front, a legitimate businessman. He opened a sundries store called "Alfie's" on Alton Road—"open all night."

In fact, he had a concession in the bag to open another "Alfie's" store at the new, postwar Miami International Airport, but a bit of untimely—and unfavorable—publicity caused the Airport Authority to reassess Alfie's qualifications. It seems a couple of conniving newsmen placed bets with the entrepeneur in the Commodore Hotel room that was headquarters for most of his bookmaking activities. Immediately they betrayed him by publishing all the details in the morning edition of their paper, and Miami Beach police dropped by to pick up the evidence.

Again, S. & G. lawyer Ben Cohen got Alfie off the hook. The defense was the soul of simplicity: the cops who made the bust had the wrong room number on their search warrant. "Something Fishy on the Beach," newspaper headlines might have commented.

Busted for Selling Pornographic Materials

After a nearly trouble-free decade of bookmaking, Alfie was busted again in 1960. This time the state's attorney tried to prosecute him for mob ties, but ended up charging only that he sold pornographic materials off the magazine rack in his sundries store—which almost everyone knew all along. But the records show the state failed to prove it. Once more, Alfie went unpunished.

Another five years passed before the law got on Alfie's case again, and this time it was the long arm of the FBI that draped around his shoulders. J. Edgar Hoover was after interstate racketeering, and he thought he could tie Alfie to a nationwide gambling ring operating as the "Derby Sports Book." In Las Vegas, a federal grand jury included Alfie in its lengthy list of suspects indicted for racketeering, but the FBI lost the case. Alfie swore he was a total stranger to the Las Vegas gambling scene, clinging to his "hometown boy" image to the end.

Persuaded by a Bomb

Finally a well-placed bomb put a violent end to the sundries business, and Alfie announced he was ready to slow the pace a bit. It was rumored that the bombing was the work of a Chicago mobster seeking revenge because of a dispute over Alfie's gambling territory. No one knew whether the blast was designed to frighten

171

him into early retirement or kill him outright. To Alfie, it didn't matter which. He had acquired enough of the wisdom of the street to know that mobsters get what they want. Their message to Mr. Mart was that they wanted uncontested control of the lucrative bookmaking rackets in America's major cities.

Those who knew Alfie best, however, chuckled at the suggestion that he no longer "made book." The stakes were too high for anyone accustomed to Alfie's kind of income to voluntarily step aside—mob or no mob. There were, after all, ways to negotiate the matter of territories. Compromise was better than out-and-out defeat. There is no indication Alfie ever gave serious thought to early retirement.

A month after the sundries store closed, "Alfie's Tours" opened its new offices on Alton Road. The agency sold tours to Las Vegas. Fruit vendor John "Peanuts" Tronolone, another Beach gambling kingpin who also had experienced a few busts in the course of his career, popped up as Alfie's partner. The two entrepeneurs chartered flights to the Riviera Hotel in Las Vegas. Their clients were selected citizens with big bucks to donate to Nevada gambling casinos.

In Nevada, "Nobody Ever Smiles"

Alfie says he never really cared much about Nevada, however. He compares it with a place "hit by a nuclear bomb or something." His real complaint: "Nobody ever smiles there." Alfie likes for people to smile. His share of the tours business finally ended up in the hands of Hymie Lazar, allegedly an associate of suspected underworld financier Meyer Lansky.

"He still must be handling well over 100 million a year in bets," one law enforcement official conjectured recently, "and that means Alfie's personal take has to be something like 5 million bucks each year."[4] Whatever the accommodation made with the mobsters, Alfie apparently negotiated a deal he and they could live with—and handsomely.

But in 1976, a special statewide grand jury inquired into Alfie's activities once again. Undercover cops had made home movies showing him in suspiciously clandestine conversation with a Beach police major. Police Chief Pomerance persuaded the officer to retire. The grand jury promptly returned indictments on 99 counts of illicit gambling against the legendary Miami Beach bookie. This time there appeared to be enough evidence to "put him away for at least 25 years."[5]

It still was not to be, however. Whoever wrote the indictments failed to specify that Alfie's operation took in territory beyond Dade County. Only a technicality, to be sure, but after the S. & G. attorneys finished with the oversight all the charges were dropped. Strange, isn't it, how often our law enforcement process can roll over and play dead when big bucks give the orders?

Convincing Evidence on a Tape Recording

Not yet ready to accept defeat, Major Fred Woodridge of the Miami Beach Police Department worked out a new and more surreptitious strategy. He arranged for one of Alfie's regular customers to tape record their conversation as he placed an illegal bet with the bookmaker. The taped conversation came through loud, clear and incriminating. When the tape was delivered to

173

Major Woodridge, the evidence of Alfie's guilt seemed irrefutable. The police were confident they had him at last, with all avenues of escape effectively blocked.

What they had not counted on, however, was the shaky character—the world-class greed—of their witness. Sensing that an opportunity even more golden lay before him if he played his cards craftily, the informant got in touch secretly with Alfie and offered to drop out of sight for a mere $7,500. No witness; no conviction—it would be just that simple.

And Alfie was his usual giant step ahead. He took this new turn of events to the FBI—right over the heads of the Miami Beach police. The G-men had no choice but to arrest the scheming informant on charges of extortion—and there, of course, went the case against Mr. Mart. The credibility of the witness had been destroyed. After that, Alfie managed to keep his name out of the newspapers for nearly a decade. He took his activities underground.

No Longer "Untouchable"

He came to terms with the fact that bookmaking in Miami Beach is no longer the wide-open, virtually untouchable enterprise it once was. He did such a convincing disappearing act that some vice squad officers assumed he was dead.

Several hundred wagering customers, however, kept in touch. "The man is real good at what he does," observed a lifelong Miami Beach resident who admitted he places "a little bet now and then—but only when it's a sure thing." From his new secret base, Alfie knew his bettors by their voices. He used his phenomenal agility with numbers and his awesome memory recall to the best possible advantage.

Though more than 70 years of age, Alfie still can compete with an office calculator in his swift, accurate, off-the-top-of-the-head computing of odds in a race or a sports contest. In his heyday, Alfie balanced the win and lose bets in his books so skillfully that, as he skimmed his commission off the top, he is said to have pocketed as much as $100,000 a week.

"Nice Guys" Drive Their
Customers More Deeply into Debt

"The man has a computer in his head," says Florida Department of Law Enforcement gambling expert David Green. Green recognizes that another of Alfie's gifts—the ability to exude warmth, caring and trust— also enhances considerably his professional expertise. "He really does come across as a nice guy," Green concedes. "But then all successful bookies must come across as nice guys. That image makes it easier for them to drag their customers deeper and deeper into debt."[6]

Recently, Miami Beach police stumbled on Alfie's still-flourishing operation while tracking down a different lead altogether, and the word got around that it was time for Mr. Mart to be put out of business for keeps. Forty years is long enough. Sgt. Mike Klein got a court order from Dade Circuit Judge Herbert Klein authorizing a wiretap on Alfie's telephones. The police put a tail on him the clock around.

The seasoned old bookie followed a daily regimen that would do credit to an ambitious young business

175

executive half his age. He left his three-bedroom home in exclusive Bay Harbor Islands promptly at nine each morning, dressed in the blue pullover sweatshirt that over the years had become his trademark. He boarded his six-year-old Ford station wagon and drove to a down-stairs apartment on Lincoln Terrace. There, aided by three assistants, he began answering calls from a bank of telephones. The calls came in through a complicated forwarding system that made it virtually impossible for anyone to discover his location. After a brief lunch break over a take-out sandwich and a Coke from the Epicure, he would spend the rest of the afternoon on the tele-phones again.

Quick Decisions amid
Rapidly Changing Odds

Police records indicate Alfie often worked three tele-phones himself, always employing that computer brain to balance his book and make the quick decisions required in the world of rapidly changing odds. No one ever used a name outsiders might recognize. But Alfie knew the code names and the voices as well, and if he didn't know them the conversation was brought to an abrupt end. To avoid the risk of confusion, no two names were alike. There was "the doctor," "the lawyer" and "the major." "Milty" was a frequent caller, and there were dozens of other first names and nicknames.

The investigation dragged out over many months because vice squad people wanted to close every loop-hole. Then, after a brisk Super Bowl betting spree, Alfie learned the boom was being lowered at last. Beach police stormed the Lincoln Terrace apartment and carried away large boxes filled with incriminating evidence.

Racketeering and Bookmaking Charges for Alfie and His Son

On November 15, 1984, Mart and 16 of his associates—plus their 13 lawyers—surrendered themselves to Judge Marie Korvick at the Dade County Circuit Court on charges of racketeering and 18 counts of bookmaking. One of the associates arrested was Alfie's by-that-time 35-year-old son—the former star quarterback. For the court appearance, the white-haired, bearded patriarch diplomatically exchanged his blue sweatshirt for a dark business suit. Four additional suspects, now living in other states, agreed to surrender later that month. Two gentlemen named Nick Sklaroff and Louis Sitaras refused to cooperate, and Assistant State Attorney Ben Daniel said they would be sought as fugitives.

Police claim they have information linking the legendary "nice guy" with the Colombo Family in New York, along with organized crime figures in Las Vegas, Chicago and New Jersey. His private empire apparently has reached far beyond the now deteriorating beach community in which it had its origin and where it grew and prospered. The empire probably embraces even the kingpins who tried to bomb him out of business a couple of decades ago.

And how does Mr. Mart feel about all that? Not exactly the kind of repentance one might hope for. In fact, to Alfie's way of thinking, neither a lawmaker nor a law enforcer in our country would recognize an honest or an innocent man "if one bit him on the leg."

177

An Ethical System Uniquely His Own

Alfie lives by an ethical system uniquely his own. "The gambler's business is the most honorable of all," he insists. "In the so-called legitimate businesses you have lawyers, contracts, checks, periods, dotted lines— and a complete lack of trust. And you have plenty of cheating."

And what about *your* business, Mr. Mart?

"In my business it's like when two gentlemen sit down to a game of poker," Alfie says. "There it is your word and the other person's word. What it really comes down to is reputation. What it really comes down to is honor."[7]

Mr. Mart may not be aware of Ralph Waldo Emerson's astute observation in one of his essays more than a century ago. "The louder he talked of his honor," wrote the outspoken Bostonian, "the faster we counted our spoons."[8] It sounds now as if the spoon count in Miami Beach finally has begun.

Points to Ponder

1. When you read that someone ran a highly visible bookie operation for 30 years in the same location, do you (a) take for granted, (b) assume, (c) suspect or perhaps (d) doubt seriously that he did so with police knowledge and maybe even the protection of

178

law enforcement people? If you were a police officer and a believer in Jesus Christ, how would you deal with the appearance of evil involved here?

2. How do you feel about Alfie Mart's comment that Miami Beach cops "should be out catching criminals"? Should law enforcement officers establish priorities for types of crime more despicable or more harmful than gambling and concentrate on those rather than on enforcing vice laws?

3. How could mobsters in Chicago possibly get interested in a bookmaking operation in faraway Miami Beach? Do you think there really is a conspiracy properly known as "organized crime"? Should the fact that crime already is a costly reality cause us to lower our guard against or lessen our efforts to keep organized crime out of our communities?

4. In our eagerness to protect constitutional rights, have we made it too easy for law violators to avoid punishment for their crimes? What about the possibility of an innocent person being punished unjustly? Would you testify against someone on trial for mugging you without being sure beyond all doubt you could identify him as the guilty person?

5. Is there truth in the old adage that there is "honor among thieves"? How do you feel about Alfie's claim that "the gambler's business is the most honorable of all," a business in which thousands of dollars change hands constantly on the basis of a handshake and a verbal agreement? If Alfie had a disastrously bad week, losing far more bets than he won, forcing him to the edge of bankruptcy, do you feel you could trust him implicitly to pay you the $5,000 you won? When?

Notes

1. *Miami Herald,* November 15, 1984, sect. D, p. 1.
2. Ibid., sect. D, p. 12.
3. Ibid.
4. Anonymous police officer in personal interview with the author, November 17, 1985.
5. *Miami Herald,* November 15, 1984, sect. D, p. 12.
6. Telephone conversation with author, November 25, 1984.
7. *Miami Herald,* sect. D, p. 12.
8. John Bartlett, *Bartlett's Familiar Quotations,* 15th ed. (Boston: Little, Brown and Company, 1980), p. 488: n. 1.

13
Enforcement of Gambling Laws

ONE OF THE FACTS of life that permits people like Alfie Mart to operate unmolested is that people who enforce gambling laws do not always operate on the same wavelength as the public or the people who make the laws.

"Until the management of the prosecutorial and judicial systems is changed," warns the National Institute of Law Enforcement and Criminal Justice, "it appears to us that decisions by the legislatures about how to treat various kinds of gambling offenders will be largely irrelevant to what actually happens . . . . Legislators must address the way that enforcement is managed both by police and by prosecutors."[1]

Why? Because without enforcement and adequate punitive measures, merely making laws inevitably proves a governmental exercise in futility. That is why the values, the priorities, the personal commitment and the integrity of law enforcement officers, prosecutors and judges are of overwhelming importance in the maintaining of law and order.

A Struggle Between Conscience and Expediency

Where gambling is concerned, judicial attitudes—like the attitudes of the public—appear to be changing. The result? A nation locked in a struggle between conscience and expediency. And you can count on the pendulum to swing rapidly in the direction of expediency, unless some powerful force for morality takes the initiative.

Who will do it? That's where you and I come in. For if anyone is going to do it, we Christians must lead in a new assessment concerning the benign or malignant qualities of gambling operations and the appropriate punishment, if any, for law violations.

State legislators across the nation must be made aware of these four compellingly urgent questions:

1. *Should more commercial gambling be made legal?*

The issue has various challenging aspects, including the moral, the ethical, the economic and the psychological. Among the most intriguing of these aspects are largely untested speculations concerning the reliability of law enforcement. Lawmakers are uncertain of the possible impact of even limited legalized gambling on the enforcement of whatever antigambling laws may be retained.

2. *Should certain forms of social gambling be decriminalized?*

Moral considerations lie always beyond the mere mechanics of research findings, but some lawmakers are probing deeply into the nature of current gambling laws and restudying the reasons for the existence of these restrictions. Laws prohibiting social gambling characteristically are unenforced and generally considered unenforceable. What, then, is their value?

Enforcement people suggest the primary value of such laws is their potential use in breaking up commercial gambling operations that *claim* to be harmless social activities. Lawmakers are analyzing the kind of responsibility placed on police officers by usually impractical laws against social gambling and inquiring into the ways and reasons some are enforced while others are ignored.

3. *Should harsher penalties be set for serious gambling offenders?*

Should legislatures mandate more severe penalties for, say, convicted bookies, just as they do for armed robbery felons and other perpetrators of crimes considered unusually dangerous? The issues are frustratingly complex. Few lawmakers claim to have developed more than a superficial or theoretical understanding of the significance of current penalties—either as punitive measures or as deterrents.

4. *Is illegal gambling, after all, rightly classified among "victimless" crimes?*

Violators of such laws characteristically receive more lenient treatment when brought before the court. But

183

before our judicial system exonerates the bookie or the numbers racketeer on "victimless" grounds, another question demands an answer. What of dependents deprived of necessities of life because financial resources were recklessly wasted by the addicted gambler to whom they look as family provider? What about white-collar crime, escalating because someone must recoup a loss or pay off a gambling debt?

Are not deprived families and defrauded businesses often the true "victims" when antigambling laws are trampled under foot? And what about the compulsive gambler himself? Should he be pitied or should he be punished? To the degree that his psychological illness may render him genuinely not responsible for his actions, might not he, himself, be classified, then, as a "victim"?

Enforcement Policies Are Unclear

In 1978, U.S. Department of Justice agents Floyd J. Fowler, Jr., Thomas W. Mangione and Frederick E. Pratter conducted an extensive study of enforcement patterns for the department's National Institute of Law Enforcement and Criminal Justice. They expanded considerably on earlier findings suggesting widespread uncertainty among law enforcement officers as to their responsibility where illegal gambling is known to be taking place. The agents found 60 percent of all police officers in agreement that their departmental policies concerning the enforcement of gambling laws were unclear. Most of these, in fact, were able to point out what they classified as "gross inconsistencies" in the ways their enforcement programs were administered.

184

The surveyers questioned police officers in 16 cities with populations in excess of 250,000 and learned that law enforcement officials tend to rank taking bets on sports and numbers among the least serious crimes they deal with. Illegal commercial gambling, in the words of a summary titled *Gambling Law Enforcement in Major American Cities,* is generally considered by police to be "less serious than prostitution and about on a par with after-hours liquor violations."[2]

Public Perception Is Fickle

The perceptions of the public are generally much the same as those of law enforcement officers. Several national surveys have indicated that public acceptance of legal gambling seems to follow legislative lead. That means even where sentiment is largely against activities like casinos and state lotteries, citizens will move toward acceptance once a particular kind of gambling has been approved by their lawmakers.

Majority segments of our population—more specifically, white Anglos—often are found opposing permissive gambling policies prior to legalization, but soon shifting to support once legislative approval is an accomplished fact. Lawmakers appear to exploit a wide latitude in this area. In a sense, they are allowed to act as public conscience. In the end, those who elected them to office probably will accept their decision as being "right," and seldom insist upon rethinking or review. In due time, the public can be expected to adapt to the new reality, whatever it may be. People who vote against a lottery in their state have been found among the first in line to buy Lotto tickets once the plan is implemented.

Often the public runs ahead of lawmakers in the matter of permissiveness. Two studies made within the last decade in Washington, D.C., confirm that police officials in the nation's capital feel they get inadequate support from District of Columbia citizens in the enforcement of gambling laws. They complain they are stuck with a legal albatross; they get little credit if they do a good job but a lot of abuse if they fail.

Most Suspect Police Complicity

Nearly 80 percent of all Americans are convinced that "bookies have to bribe police in order to stay in business." They feel it is not likely such illegal operations would be able to exist without the knowledge and consent of the police. Only 60 percent of those surveyed feel police would act on a gambling complaint if a citizen made one—voicing the opinion that drug dealing or fencing of stolen goods would have a much higher priority.[3]

When police are lax in their enforcement of gambling laws—or any other laws, for that matter—they risk losing the confidence of the people of their community. When citizens know that illegal gambling is taking place on their own turf, they conclude almost inevitably that their police are inept or corrupt—or both. For the police, it's a classical catch-22. They have little to gain from effective enforcement of gambling laws, considering the low priority that rates with many citizens, but they have a great deal to *lose* if they fail to live up to public expectations.

Where citizens suspect that law enforcement officers are collaborating with gambling entrepeneurs, in fact,

186

the attitude of the public becomes more demanding. When suspicion is aroused, people begin to clamor that their gambling laws be enforced.

A strange inconsistency has been revealed in the public's views concerning the enforcement of gambling laws. The findings of one survey indicate that 80 percent of all American adults feel those who accept illegal bets should be arrested—yet only 45 percent felt such people, if convicted, should be handed jail sentences. Overall, only 40 percent of American adults characterize the enforcement of gambling laws as being "very important," while 20 percent place it in a "not very important" category.[4]

Gambling Operations Linked to Organized Crime

Yet the Department of Justice has determined that two-thirds of all Americans believe revenue from illegal gambling ultimately goes to support more serious crimes such as loan-sharking and drug sales. An even greater percentage of the police officers themselves—some 80 percent—confirm that belief. Most law enforcement officers theorize that gambling operations usually have a link of some kind with organized crime. They are convinced that the long arm of the mob is able to reach into whatever area it chooses, and that the megabucks aspect of gambling operations make that profession a logical target.[5]

The Police Guide on Organized Crime, prepared for the use of law enforcement officers by the Technical Assistance Division of the Law Enforcement Assistance Administration, comments:

Gambling activity is the most serious form of organized crime. This activity supplies the financial grease that lubricates the machinery of other operations, such as importation of narcotics, penetration of legitimate business, corruption of officials, and so on.[6]

This is not the statement of a religious or moralistic antigambling vigilante group; it is the statement of an objective and responsible agency of the United States government. It is strange, though, how readily the advocates of legalized gambling scoff at such statements and brand them the mouthings of church fundamentalists or radical do-gooders out of touch with the realities of life.

The Mob and the Megabucks

There is, admittedly, considerable ambiguity in the use of the phrase "organized crime." It can be misleading at best and dangerous at worst to use it as a coverall phrase, referring to stereotyped shadowy figures from the underworld who have Italian names, wear shoulder holsters and ride in black limousines.

The Department of Justice warns, however, against underestimating the significance of organized crime on the American gambling scene or of ignoring the threat of those malignant forces in cities where they function. There can be little doubt as to the importance of gambling revenues to "the mob," whatever criminal conspiracy the term might include, or wherever the mobsters might be operating. The reason is the megabucks.

Gambling profits are big money and easy money, and that is precisely what organized crime is looking for.

And beyond the direct revenue from gambling—amounts of money so huge that the average citizen finds it difficult to grasp the significance of these statistics—is the revenue organized crime can realize from selling to bookies wire services, layoff services and other peripheral services necessary to their trade. Next are the incredibly steep interest rates charged by the loan shark, who seems seldom beyond the bookie's beck and call. The mob-related loan shark sinks his teeth into the hapless gambling loser and feeds on his losses. He has in his corner tough and merciless henchmen who can resolve quickly and efficiently any problems of collection. Since the shylock lender is not directly involved in the bookmaking, he is free of potentially culpable business connections with those who made off with the pigeon's money in the first place.

Though police officials usually place keeping revenue out of the hands of organized crime high on their list of law enforcement priorities, actual operational records do not confirm that priority. The Fowler-Mangione-Pratter report says "virtually no bookmaking arrests" had been made in nine of 16 major cities known to be fertile fields for illegal bookmakers and assumed to be infiltrated by organized crime. "Over half the departments in the sample were not aggressively enforcing laws against commercial gambling operators," the report charges.[7]

The Courts Fail to Provide Support

Police officers know painfully well that law enforcement involves more than vice squads, undercover work, sting operations and arrests. Without similar commitment on the part of prosecutors, judges and juries, the police can exercise relatively little control over illicit gambling operations. In general, police feel the courts fail to give them adequate support where gambling violations are concerned.

Their complaint is not against conviction rates. There seems to be general agreement between police, prosecutors and judges as to what constitutes a good case against a bookie or a numbers racketeer. Convictions run in excess of 70 percent of arrests made in the cities surveyed. The problem lies in what happens in the actual disposition of a case, even though a guilty verdict has been reached. Sometimes "guilty" is a mere technicality.

After an arrest is made, the police bow out and the prosecutor becomes the most important link in the chain of criminal justice. Court records suggest that not many gambling cases actually result in a trial of fact. Most cases are disposed of with a plea of some sort— "guilty" or "no contest"—or the defendants and their attorneys plea-bargain. Plea bargaining takes place when, in return for sparing the courts the expense of a trial, defendants accept a charge of less severity, thereby winning a lighter sentence.

Throughout the entire procedure, the prosecutor is the central figure. He decides whether to try the case or not, what charges to file, whether to settle for a misdemeanor or to go for a felony charge, whether to plea bargain or not and what penalty to recommend to the court.

The Role of the Judge Often Is Passive

That judges play a relatively passive role in the enforcement of gambling laws may seem ironic. In many of the cases, the defendant pleads guilty, the prosecutor recommends the penalty agreed upon in the plea-bargaining process and the judge simply imposes that sentence.

Only three kinds of sentences can put a bookmaker or numbers operator out of business: jail, a ruinously large fine or carefully supervised probation under the threat of a stiff sentence for noncompliance. Case records indicate, however, that the most common penalty after conviction for illegal commercial gambling is an astonishingly modest fine—on the average, less than $200. A fine in that range constitutes for the established professional gambling operator little more than a slap on the wrist, probably providing more cause for amusement than deterrent against further violations.

Illegal Gambling Goes on Undiminished

Some proponents insist that legalizing certain forms of commercial gambling—particularly placing these under the control of the state—will dramatically reduce the number of illegal gambling operations. The Fowler-Mangione-Pratter report, however, fails to support this theory.

"Increasing the number of available legal gambling options has not been shown to reduce illegal gambling," the agents contend. Their findings indicate that legalized gambling would have to be offered in packages providing specific and competitive alternatives to numbers

191

betting, off-track horse race and dog race wagering and sports betting, all in the exciting emotional environment offered by the illegal gambling enterprises.[8]

The problem is not that people simply like to bet; it is that individual people who place bets like to do it in a certain way and under certain circumstances—even with certain people. Substituting a legal state lottery, for example, in place of a bet on your Super Bowl favorite placed with the neighborhood bookie who calls you by your first name, simply does not provide the emotional stimulation the seasoned wagerer requires.

Permissiveness Is Gaining Momentum

Through the democratic process, legislatures in some states have decided to allow models of limited legalized gambling, and the permissive movement is gaining momentum across the country. The inconsistency of this trend lies in the fact that betting is permitted when it is done by certain people with certain other people on certain outcomes of certain contests or choices, while in other cases it is prohibited.

Americans have entrusted to their local police, prosecutors and judges the responsibility for finding, apprehending, convicting and punishing those who operate in defiance of the laws of the land. Yet it cannot be denied that in most American communities professionals enjoying apparent immunity are involved openly in gambling operations that blatantly violate the codes of their municipality and the statutes of their state. Further, it is estimated that a significant number of adult Americans break the law with impunity by routinely placing illegal bets on horses, dogs, numbers and sports events.

Needed: an Authentic Consensus
Among Christians

The gambling dilemma in our nation is formidable, and workable solutions are complex and difficult to come by. One troublesome problem is the apparent absence of an authentic, consistent and reliable consensus. Opinions concerning the rightness or wrongness of gambling tend to change in both directions as new evidence or new experience comes to light. But we will do well not to let our public servants—police, prosecutors, judges or legislators—forget that their accountability is to us, not to their own whims.

Gambling is a human indulgence with an impressive history of excesses, abuses and judicial compromise. It may be that only Christians, united in the common bond of the Christ-life they share, can take an effective initiative in resisting this corrupting trend. We may not understand clearly all the implications, but we know that as believers we are not to "trust in uncertain riches, but in the living God, who giveth us richly all things to enjoy" (1 Tim. 6:17).

Apart from our united voice, there may be no force in America capable—or even desirous—of turning the tide.

1. In maintaining law and order in this country, who do you feel has the most important assignment: those who make the laws, those who enforce them or those whose job is to prosecute law violators? In what way might conflict of interest undermine the integrity of any of the three?

2. Suppose, for example, you were a law enforcement officer—and, yes, a Christian—who considers prostitution a crime but does not "see any real harm" in gambling. Do you feel as a cop you might come down hard on violators of antiprostitution laws but be tempted to overlook violations when gambling laws are flouted? What would your Christian duty be?

3. Do you agree that the pendulum of public opinion and policy seems to be swinging in the direction of permissiveness? It is true that certain customs and attitudes are cultural and tend to change with the times, but are there well-defined concepts of right and wrong—moral absolutes—that are not subject to change? If so, how do we determine what these unchanging standards are?

4. Would you classify illegal gambling as a "victimless crime"? By what line of reasoning does someone figure he can "spare" a large amount of money if he loses it in a gambling casino or a poker game? How much money do you figure you could "spare" before you began to regret your foolhardiness in betting it?

5. Some 80 percent of all American adults feel gambling racketeers should be arrested, but only 45 per-

cent feel they should be given jail sentences. What do you feel is an appropriate penalty for convicting gambling racketeers? Do you agree with 80 percent of America's law enforcement officers that revenue from illegal gambling ultimately goes to support more serious crimes such as loan-sharking and drug sales? Do you think stiffer jail sentences would help control that tragic picture?

Notes
1. U.S. Department of Justice, National Institute of Law Enforcement and Criminal Justice, September 1978.
2. U.S. Department of Justice, Law Enforcement Assistance Administration, National Institute of Law Enforcement and Criminal Justice, *Gambling Law Enforcement in Major American Cities.* Report prepared by Floyd J. Fowler, Jr., Thomas W. Mangione and Frederick E. Pratter (Washington, DC: Government Printing Office, 1978).
3. Ibid., p. 33.
4. *Pennsylvania Crime Commission Report.* 1974.
5. *Gambling Law Enforcement,* p. 36.
6. U.S. Department of Justice, Law Enforcement Assistance Administration, Technical Assistance Division, *The Police Guide on Organized Crime* (Washington, DC: Government Printing Office, 1978), p. 32.
7. *Gambling Law Enforcement,* p. 38.
8. Ibid., p. 58.

14

Gambling as a Sickness

THE DOWNFALL of Alex Ivanovitch began when he placed 20 gold coins on "pass" at the roulette table and doubled his money. Excited by that stroke of good fortune, he tried again and won again—and tried yet another time and won yet again. In fact, he parlayed his 20 coins into 160 pieces of gold in less than five minutes. In so little time and with so little effort, he raked in a cool 800 percent return on his initial investment.

Chilled with Terror

"I was as though in delirium," Alex describes the experience, "and I moved the whole heap of gold to 'red.' All that time I was playing, I felt chilled with terror, and a shudder made my arms and legs tremble. I realized with horror what losing would mean for me now. My whole life was at stake."

But Alex did not lose—at least, not then. His luck was astonishing. He felt as if some benevolent force guided his hand in the bets he placed each time the wheel was turned. In less than half an hour he heard, as if in a trance, the croupier telling him he had reached the

30,000 florin limit allowed at any one table.

Quickly, he transferred his operation to another. There, his streak of luck continued. Soon he had pocketed the maximum allowed at the second wheel, and had moved his newly gained fortune to a different type of game where the limit on winnings was less restricting.

Intense Craving for Risk

"I was experiencing an overwhelming enjoyment in scooping up and taking away the banknotes which grew up in a heap before me," Alex reflects. "It seemed as though fate was urging me on. I am convinced that vanity was half responsible for it; I wanted to impress the spectators by taking mad risks. And—oh, the strange sensation! I remember distinctly that, quite apart from the promptings of vanity, I was pressured by an intense craving for risk.

"Perhaps passing through so many sensations, my soul was not satisfied, but only irritated by them, and craved still more sensations—and stronger and stronger ones till utterly exhausted."

Alex's total winnings for the evening: 100,000 florins. He was, at that moment, a very wealthy man!

"You are bold—very bold," two solemn observers said to him at the door as he marched triumphantly from the casino floor. "But be sure to go away tomorrow as soon as possible, or else you will lose it all—you will lose it *all*."

The next day, Ivanovitch did in fact leave the city— and that only because of previous plans that could not be changed. In due time, though, the lure of the games brought him to the casino again, lusting after more

198

excitement and greater riches. Whereupon the solemn prophecy heard at the door became a grim and depressing reality. He did indeed lose it *all*.

The Loss Spurs Him On

But somehow that loss served only to quicken his pulse, narrow his vision and enlarge his enthusiasm for the chase. He was determined to recover from the temporary setback and become once again the wealthy, self-assured and much envied man the casino had made him on his first visit.

From that point on, the life of Alex Ivanovitch was never the same. With even the smallest amount of cash in his pockets, he returned to the gaming rooms, eager to experience those sensations of risk, of power, of despair, of triumph and of desperate anticipation.

"I am living, of course, in continual anxiety," the now compulsive gambler testified. "I play for the tiniest stakes, and I keep waiting for something, calculating, standing for whole days at the gambling table, and watching for the play. I even dream of playing. But I feel that in all this I have, as it were, grown stiff and wooden, as though I had sunk into a muddy swamp.

"Can I fail to understand that I am a lost man? But—can I not rise again? Yes, I have only for once in my life to be prudent and patient. I have only for once to show will power, and in one hour I can transform my destiny. The greatest thing is will power!"

"Tomorrow It Will All Be Over"

It seemed as simple as that. But for Alex Ivanovitch

that simple solution of will power never materialized. And thus his painful dilemma remains unresolved at the close of Fyodor Dostoevsky's depressing book titled, *The Gambler.* The story ends with Alex's despairing sigh, "Tomorrow—tomorrow it will all be over!"[1]

Dostoevsky's tragic novel is assumed to be an autobiographical account of his own personal slavery to the gaming tables, written more than a century ago. The celebrated Russian author of *The Brothers Karamazov* was himself a compulsive gambler—one of the most notorious of his day. The gifted novelist wrote great books partly because he needed royalties to cover his losses in the casinos of Europe. The fictitious Alex doubtless testifies to the sensations Dostoesvsky himself experienced in those terrifying moments when he discovered he was no longer in control of his own will—and thus of his destiny. He was never quite sure after that discovery whether or not life was worth the effort.

Clement McQuaid, who assembled the exhaustive study of games and gamers titled *Gamblers Digest,* takes issue with the old cliche that "all gamblers die broke." It is more accurate to say, he insists, that they *live* broke—that their personal agony is the necessity of going on living in financial ruin and relentless shame, existing from one scam or fraud or broken promise to the next.[2]

They All Die Broke

"Our extensive research has shown that compulsive, psychotic gamblers go broke well *before* the end of their lives unless something is done to stop them," McQuaid notes. He documents case after case establishing what appears to be a universal truth: unskilled, uninformed, desperate, bet-for-the-fun-of-it or gamble-to-make-a-fast-buck rollers almost without exception prove to be losers. And that pattern usually becomes evident quite early in their careers.

The personal tragedy stalking the compulsive gambler can be just as ruinous and painful as that associated with compulsive drinking or other addictions. Money lost at the gaming table or to the neighborhood bookie means hard work gone to waste, loved ones penalized, careers ruined, hopes and dreams crushed and financial security sacrificed forever. Promising lives—even entire families—have suffered devastating and irretrievable loss on the roll of the dice, the turn of the wheel, the numbers on a card or the chance outcome of a sporting event.

$35 Billion in Insurance Fraud Losses

Dr. Henry Lesieur, a professor of sociology at St. John's University in New York City, has completed a study of the relationships between compulsive gambling and crime, and his findings are sobering. Lesieur concludes that the nation's millions—authorities differ on how many—of pathological gamblers may be responsible for more than $35 billion in insurance fraud losses spread over their lifetimes. The insurance money they claim on bogus losses is used to pay off gambling debts. Interpreted conservatively, that figure suggests an insurance fraud extortion of at least $1 billion each year, attributable directly to the recouping of gambling losses. That is a formidable penalty to be inflicted upon the public through the frantic efforts of compulsive gamblers to get back into the action again.[3]

Other surveys also have sought to determine what percentage of gamblers resort to illegal means in order to recoup those losses. It is questionable how precise the following figures are when applied to the total spectrum of addicted gamblers, but they do suggest a frightening relationship between gambling losses and white collar crime:

Sixty-six percent of identified compulsive gamblers interviewed in several surveys admitted to embezzling company money.

Forty-three percent said they had resorted to writing worthless checks to make the payoff.

Thirty-two percent admitted they had filed false auto accident claims to collect insurance.

Seventeen percent described various means of tax fraud they had attempted.

Fifteen percent acknowledged faking a business or home burglary to collect insurance.

Eleven percent said they had been involved in arson in order to acquire money.[4]

Treat Them or Punish Them?

Through the years, society has been hard pressed to

determine how it should regard or treat compulsive gamblers. Are these people afflicted with a treatable illness that deserves sympathy and clinical help, or are they merely moral weaklings to be censured and disciplined? Only in relatively recent years have psychologists progressed toward a clearer understanding of what compels people to do things which, in their more thoughtful moments, they determine—however futilely—not to do again.

Compulsion of one kind or another probably is a weakness afflicting every member of the human race. Compulsion is a functional flaw in our fallen nature. Doubtless all of us experience from time to time that strong, irresistible, yet often subconscious desire to do or say or indulge in something admittedly not in our best interest—even if it is something no more ominous than being a chocoholic.

Compulsions come in assorted sizes and shapes, and with various degrees of significance and threat. We encounter compulsion probably most routinely and dramatically in the area of narcotics and alcohol, but humans experience addiction in many other ways worthy of concern. We might experience some serious soul-searching before denying occasional struggles in the area of lying, stealing, cheating, talking too much, extramarital sex, overeating, gossiping, twitching, nail biting or, perhaps, something as inocuous as giggling when there is nothing really funny to cause our amusement.

A Uniquely Devastating Kind of Grief

Compulsive gamblers, however, inflict upon family members, friends and business associates a uniquely devastating brand of frustration and grief. They are likely to risk their reputations, their family's comfort and security, their life savings, their future, their jobs, their freedom or their personal safety on the turn of a card, the roll of the dice or the speed of an animal at the racetrack or the kennel club. In "The Celebrated Jumping Frog," Mark Twain described the local gambling enthusiast this way: "If there was two birds sitting on a fence, he would bet you which one would fly first."[5]

For people like that, gambling is no longer recreation—often not even a source of personal enjoyment. It is a loathsome pathological obsession. It is a cruel and relentless master. Compulsive gamblers suffer from an identifiable dysfunction of the mental processes.

Probably there is no cure—at least not apart from something almost metaphysical that provides the victim with a consuming desire to be well again. A genuine spiritual rebirth might provide the solution, but only if it is followed by a determined process of learning and maturing. Whatever the therapy, the only gambling addict who can hope for deliverance from this bondage is one who faces squarely the implications of his sickness and takes the drastic steps necessary to bring it under control.

The urge to gamble on something—preoccupation with wagering either to win or to lose—expands in the awareness of its victim until it becomes a substitute for reality. The interests of family, health, friendships, business and financial stability are overshadowed by the irrational compulsion to bet on something. What matters most is what gamblers think of as "the action." As one compulsive gambler put it, "The next best thing to

gambling and winning probably is gambling and losing."

Once He Was Considered
Stupid and Irresponsible

Dr. Robert Custer, medical advisor to the National
Council on Compulsive Gambling and designer of the
Veterans Administration's in-patient treatment programs
for addicted gamblers, points out that threats of punishment and rejection were the tools society once
attempted to use to control the person whose weakness
is gambling. His addictive behavior was considered stupid and irresponsible, and he was treated accordingly.
His calamitous loss of money, the waste of his time, tal-
ent and energies, the hardships and heartaches he
brings to dependent family members, would seem reason enough for the compulsive gambler to renounce his
weakness and mend his way. As thousands of victims
now know, it seldom turns out that way.[6]

In 1924, Dr. Ernst Simmel declared gambling to be
an effort to gain "narcissistic supplies," such as food,
love, comfort and attention—things the gambler feels
have been denied him. The Austrian psychologist classified the adult compulsive gambler as one who has
regressed to childhood. Further, he diagnosed the gambling mania as rising out of man's ingrained desire to
avoid work.[7]

A Fantasy World in Which
They Feel Important

Today that attitude is seen as an unfair judgment

205

and an unwarranted oversimplification. The prevailing view among psychologists now is that compulsive gamblers are striving to create for themselves an acceptable form of reality—a fantasy world in which they can feel important, challenged, power-wielding, influential and respected, no matter how painful or costly the process of achieving it. As the habit worsens, these pathological inner drives become even more urgent than the welfare of their dependents or the basic components of their personal financial stability.

The Veterans Administration provides a psychological profile indicating the compulsive gambler is neither stupid nor naive. Neither is he necessarily criminal. The typical addict, in fact, has superior intelligence and is vigorously competitive. He is a hard worker with a high energy level. Usually he has done well in school, likes challenges, thrives on excitement, seldom relaxes and finds boredom difficult to tolerate. Curiously, he may also display an almost stoic acceptance of the fact that the odds are against him. Unfortunately, that perception will not deter him from placing his bet and hoping for a favorable outcome anyway.

Tracing the Problem to Early Adolescence

The compulsive gambler probably can trace his wagering habits back to early adolescence—or beyond. He may have done his first serious gambling when he was still in his teens. Five years or more may have passed before he realized he had a problem, but even then he was not likely to admit it to anyone but himself.

He probably has his favorite type of gambling and sticks with it, win or lose. Compulsive gamblers are divided fairly evenly in their preference between casinos, horse races, card games and sports betting through bookies. But dog races, jai-alai, numbers games—even church bingo parties—also have their loyal devotees.

The Three Phases of Addiction

Identifying the compulsive gambler seldom is a cut-and-dried judgment, but Dr. Custer has found three phases in the development of a confirmed "gambleholic." It may be worth the effort to check the details of these phases against your own experiences, or against those of someone for whom you feel a responsibility or a concern.

In the *winning phase* of his journey toward addiction, the gambler usually experiences a stimulating "score," or an unusual run of good luck. He is pleased with this new-found source of easy money, and this encourages him to bet again. He seeks out the experts and learns the strategies. He probably develops a useful knowledge of gambling odds and risks. This qualifies him—especially in his own eyes—as an accomplished and successful gambler.

At this point, things may still be comfortably under control, and he is well able to quit while he is ahead. The lure of the game is difficult to resist, however, and the dangers of continuing are not readily apparent. The gambler is reluctant to terminate an activity he has found enjoyable and perhaps even profitable. Therefore he must continue—at least until this particular streak of luck has spent itself.

Because he is not really naive, the knowledgeable gambler understands there is no such thing as "luck" or "a lucky person." He knows the odds, given enough time, must return always to balance. But a big win establishes in his mind the fact that the kill can happen, and that therefore it just might happen again. And the sure way *not* to cash in on it is to be out of action when it falls.

The "Big Win" Gets Him Started

Winning suggests to the uninitiated person a wonderful and heretofore undiscovered solution to whatever financial problems may be plaguing him. The testimonies of many compulsive gamblers confirm that the addictive "big win" can be large enough to approximate the individual's legitimate annual income at the time. That much money is enough to make a favorable and lasting impression, and certainly it is enough to cloud any logical thought about those immutable laws of average.

Ironically, that "big win" may herald the end of the winning phase and the beginning of the *losing phase.* Now the net or the noose is being tightened, whichever metaphor seems more appropriate. It is, of course, the law of averages that is closing the gap between the wins and the losses. But that bit of rationality usually eludes the compulsive gambler, along with the obvious fact that house and track splits substantially increase the odds against him.

The indomitable winner—the dauntless, unconquerable master of his fate at the gaming table—finds his reasoning powers paralyzed by the unfavorable turn of the tide, and by the tension generated through the higher stakes now demanded. His losses soar. Funds available from former winnings are exhausted. He begins to dip into savings, to liquidate investments or to borrow informally from cronies who are more prosperous—but not more rational—than he is.

Frenzy Is the Cardinal Sin

Soon even greater losses must be recouped, and that means larger bets—perhaps against greater odds. A pattern of frenzy emerges that blurs the logic and diminishes whatever gambling skills may have been acquired. Wise and nonaddicted gamblers avoid that frenzy like smallpox. Indeed, they consider that lapse of rationality—the frenzy—the cardinal sin of their profession and the sure mark of the pathological player.

As the process of addiction continues, the search for money becomes ever more frantic, because it is ever more urgent that the action continue and that losses be recovered. Insurance policies may be cashed in, stocks sold, mortgage payments skipped, bonds liquidated, collateral loans sought. But while this availability of cash through liquidated assets or legal loans seems at the moment a boon to the anxious gambler, it is in fact another seed of his destruction.

Liquidation becomes to him the equivalent of a gambling win. It is bailout money easily and quickly available, with only routine effort involved in getting it. When he negotiates a loan, interest rates and repayment schedules seem of no great concern. He reasons that enormous gambling wins, soon and certain to come, will take care of these minor details and compensate him generously for the temporary setback.

Less Expertise and Greater Risks

Though he has, in fact, gained some useful skills at the games, under the weight of his increasing anxiety and frustration, the compulsive gambler is now becoming less expert. Further, he is taking greater risks and betting more in an effort to recoup those losses. Inner conflict for him has become a worrisome and sleepless way of life. He must bend the truth more often now, because it is important that loved ones, business associates and friends not be aware that his life is becoming unmanageable.

We have, then, a less skilled gambler, with needs growing ever greater and more urgent, risking more by betting more, with frustration mounting and with less help available, because those who might come to his rescue are kept in ignorance of his struggle. The web of deceit he continuously weaves around his frenzied activities hides the urgency of his worsening dilemma. The compulsive gambler in this losing phase becomes a veritable genius at manufacturing excuses for his often bizarre behavior. He glibly explains to his wife or to his business associates where he has been or what he was doing at the time he was expected to be somewhere else. His family is robbed of the time it is entitled to expect from him. His productivity at work diminishes because of lost time and increased preoccupation with his frustration and his financial difficulties.

Relationships deteriorate. Once the compulsive gambler's lies are exposed—and that exposure comes sooner or later—his wife, his children, his friends and his business associates experience a sense of betrayal which adds bitterness to their complaints. Their demands for a change become more angry and more insistent.

A Defensive Bitterness

The gambler responds to those demands with a defensive bitterness of his own. From his blurred point of view, this bitterness is justified because people he believes owe him trust are not providing it. People he feels should recognize his ability to handle his own affairs and make his own decisions are suggesting he is incompetent to control his finances or establish his priorities. This he sees as a final emasculation he must not tolerate.

Through all of this—or so it seems to the gambler— the solution to his problems is less complicated than others realize. Moreover, it is always imminent. The big win is the solution—even if, for the moment, that solution lies just beyond his reach. Payments on loans, stacks of unpaid bills and multiplying unmet personal obligations are seen as merely temporary inconveniences because that winning streak lies just around the next bend. When it happens, he will make everything right again—and with money to spare. Thus bigger bets seem the best assurance of large wins. The gambler is, in fact, constructing his own prison, bar by bar.

The Desperation Phase Begins

It may be difficult to determine exactly when the losing phase is over and the *desperation* phase begins, but Dr. Custer finds that final phase a phenomenon almost certain to take place. Pressure from creditors increases, further threatening the gambler's protective cloak of anonymity. When bills or dunning letters arrive in the mail, they must be intercepted and hidden from others in his family or place of employment. Elaborate explanations must be concocted to justify the "unreasonable" demands made by these creditors. By this time, the gambler's job probably is in jeopardy. His family may be suffering genuine deprivation of basic needs, and his alienation from loved ones may have become a tragic reality, shaking the very foundations of his family life.

With legal borrowing resources exhausted, the risk of loan-shark funding must be taken, and this at backbreaking interest rates. In due time, the day of reckoning comes. The embattled gambler must produce large sums of money to satisfy the credit demands of his shylocks. Failing that, he runs the risk of disgrace, blackmail, injury or death at the hands of those shadowy financiers who eventually grow weary of his empty promises to pay.

On top of all that, he may now be threatened by employment termination, divorce, the rebellion of his disillusioned children—or by all three. His world has begun to disintegrate, and he may begin to recognize his own desperation.

A Guarded Acknowledgment of Failure

A partial confession often is seen as a possible remedy at this point. So he manages a guarded acknowledgment of his failure—made to a carefully selected audience of those who, for whatever reasons, may feel responsible for the unfortunate man. "It was a crummy thing I did, and I've sure learned my lesson," he is likely to plead. "I just want you to know how sorry I am and how bad I feel about it." This may be said or written to parents, spouse, children, in-laws or more distant affluent relatives. With a special show of chagrin and self-condemnation, he makes the acknowledgment usually to those he feels may bail him out.

And frequently, someone does. Some generous sympathetic soul provides money to rescue the errant relative or friend from his uncomfortable predicament. This is done, of course, on the basis of his solemn, often tearful pledge that he will indulge no more his despicable weakness.

The bailout may, in fact, serve only to reactivate the compulsive mechanism inside the outwardly penitent man. The flaw in his bailout is that it does not require the compulsive gambler to assume responsibility for his own destructive behavior. His unwillingness to accept that responsibility is the very seed of his character weakness.

A Familiar Scenario

The scenario is not unlike what occurs when an alcoholic is bailed out of jail after his most recent arrest for driving while intoxicated. Shedding tears of repentance, he is escorted home for a hot shower and a good meal. Family members rally dutifully and loyally around to hear his solemn promise. He will banish demon rum forever from his life.

Too late, they discover he has hidden a pint of Jack Daniels under the kitchen sink!

The gambler's bailout can become, in fact, the

213

equivalent of another big win. Irrational as it may sound, the bailout serves only to reinforce the pattern of compulsion that is his undoing. He suffers further erosion of any genuine concern for himself or for those affected by his addiction. Those who provided the bailout, in the end, see no evidence of sincerity and no return on their investment. No restitution is made. Soon the benefactors are watching a repeat performance of all that destroyed both the man and his relationships the first time around. All doubt now should be banished. He is hooked. The man is a sick compulsive gambler.[8]

Where the Action Is

Central to the obsessive world of the compulsive gambler is something known as "the action." Practiced rationalizer that he is, the gambler tells himself it is essential that he be never far from where that action is. There he will capture the big win which shortly must bring an end to his agony.

In reality, it is the action itself that draws him into the vortex and keeps him spinning helplessly there—win or lose. Dostoevsky described that sensation as commitment to "the game for the game's sake."

Ernst Hoffman wrote a short story a century ago in which the lure of the action is described in these words: "To many, the game in itself presents an indescribably mysterious joy, quite without any reference to winning ... our spirits stretch their wings to reach that darksome realm, that mysterious laboratory where the Power in question works, and there see it working."

The sensation of action can be provided by a unique environment created either *for* the game or *by* the game, depending on what form of wagering the gambler has chosen. The racetrack has its own electrified ambience, supported by the murmur of tension-packed spectators and by the strident voice of the track announcer as the horses round the bend. Excitement at the racetrack is increased by rumors and by deliberately false reports which provide momentum for the surge to the betting windows.

An Ambience for the Gambler

In the casino, the theme is timelessness. There are no clocks. There is the eternal bath of flourescent lighting—the uninterrupted sensation of motion and excitement. Roulette wheels click, wheels of fortune grind, slot machines whir and crap tables provide periodic uproar as enthusiastic bettors throw their seven or make their point.

At the jai-alai fronton (arena), the atmosphere for pari-mutuel betting is strangely akin to that of the ancient Roman Colosseum. In this furious game of Basque origin—seldom found in this country outside of Florida—speed, danger and the cracking and banging of a murderously hard pelota (ball) tingle the smoke-filled arena with excitement. The ambience of the game is in ironic contrast with the "holy day" meaning of the Basque word, *jai-alai* or "merry festival."

For many compulsive gamblers, the action "high" can also be experienced far from the scene of the actual contest. Some addicts can create the necessary environment quite alone, slouched in bed or squeezed into a telephone booth in animated conversation with their bookie.

215

An Inner Loneliness and Isolation

Yet the outward confidence of the compulsive gambler often masks an inner loneliness, isolation, insecurity and desolation that slowly destroys him. He cannot handle intimacy, so he conceals his inner thoughts, hopes and fears from those who could become his deliverers. This hastens the breakdown in his personal relationships. Nothing of his secret feelings can be allowed to surface that might belie the "cool" image he wears like a costume or a mask in a play. In time, he may become unable to experience or display any legitimate emotion about anything—not even when he wins.

The confirmed compulsive gambler is trapped in a vicious cycle of anxiety, denial, survival through occasional wins, deepening indebtedness, pressure from creditors, deteriorating relationships, hidden longing for self-respect and reassurance, and a tightening ring of tension that surrounds most waking moments. From what probably began as an innocent recreational pastime, his gambling adventures have evolved into something now assuming tyrannical control of his life.

There Is No Cure

Monsignor Joseph A. Dunne, executive director of the National Council on Compulsive Gambling, says there is no cure. But he offers assurance that the disease can be arrested—or perhaps "placed in remission" is a more appropriate term. Monsignor Dunne testifies that an occasional compulsive gambler does indeed escape the clutches of the addiction through his own effort and determination. Some have succeeded in making it back to the happiness, fulfillment and purpose of a life free from betting. However, the percentage of those who make a clean getaway through their own inner resources is discouragingly low.[9]

Curiously, little has been said or done by evangelical Christians to address the problem of compulsive gambling. As far as this writer can determine, no organized effort reaches out for the betting addict that could be considered the equivalent of the rescue mission's ministry to the wino and the drifter.

A Greater Awareness of the Syndrome

The National Foundation for Study and Treatment of Pathological Gambling, located in Washington, DC, points out that while more than 4,000 treatment programs are available to our nation's estimated 9 million to 10 million alcoholics, we provide only 16 treatment programs for perhaps 4 million compulsive gamblers. The foundation hopes to correct this imbalance by creating a greater awareness of the pathological gambling syndrome. Its goal is the establishing of a national—and ultimately an international—network of residential and out-patient treatment and research facilities that will address the needs of gambling addicts.

The foundation has been instrumental in the creation of compulsive gambling treatment programs in New York, Maryland and Connecticut, and its staff members have trained participants in those remedial programs to share their healing with others. Dr. Robert L. Custer, in addition to his work with the Veterans Administration and the National Council, is president of the foundation.

Taylor Manor, in Ellicott City, Maryland, offers an intensive private treatment for compulsive gamblers with a program created by the National Foundation for the Study and Treatment of Pathological Gambling. The cost is high—somewhere in the neighborhood of $10,000 per person, with no guarantee of permanent reversal—but, then, as the wife of one of its clients asked, "How can we put a price tag on things like happiness and purpose in the life of a family?"

The Peer Support of Gamblers Anonymous

Gamblers Anonymous (GA) offers what appears to be the most readily available approach to the gambling problem, offered at no cost to anyone who will acknowledge his sickness and commit himself or herself to the healing process. GA has a significantly high success ratio with its low-key, peer-support formula, patterned after the highly successful Alcoholics Anonymous (AA) program. Given its relative youth and its lack of publicity, GA's performance is impressive and encouraging.

GA does not profess to be a "Christian solution"—not any more than AA claims any specific religious commitment. This dedicated organization has been instrumental, however, in bringing multitudes back from the brink of the dark and forbidding abyss that lies before the pathological gambler. Elementary as it may seem, the deliverance of these men and women came through the 12 simple steps that constitute the program of healing developed and administered by Gamblers Anonymous.

1. In the case of Dostoevsky's gambler, Alex Ivanovitch, do you think he developed a perception of reality that is different from our own? In your own real world, exactly what place does money hold? In what way does money relate—or not relate—to God?

2. Why do you think Dostoevsky introduced into the story the two mysterious strangers at the door of the casino who assured Ivanovitch that, if he returned the next day, he would "lose it all"? As a notorious compulsive gambler himself, had the author experienced regret that he did not accept that advice—perhaps from himself?

3. One of Ivanovitch's classical lines is "I have only for once to show will power, and in one hour I can transform my destiny. The greatest thing is will power!" Don't we all suffer now and then suffer some form of compulsion—perhaps something no more reprehensible than eating too much? What was the occasion when you last bemoaned your own lack of will power?

4. What is your view of people who cannot control their urge to gamble? Are they afflicted with an illness that needs treatment, or are they moral weaklings who need to be set straight? Do you think it is possible for a genuine Christian to be addicted to gambling—or to anything else, for that matter?

5. If most compulsive gamblers can trace their addiction back to early adolescence, what sort of stand do

you think Christian families should take regarding their children and gambling? Can we justify a double standard in this regard—that is, believers forbidding children to gamble because they are "too young," while they, the parents, indulge in card games for money, the purchase of state lottery tickets or occasional trips to gambling casinos.

Notes
1. Fyodor Dostoevsky, *The Gambler,* trans. Andrew R. MacAndrew (New York: W.W. Norton & Co., Inc., 1981).
2. Clement McQuaid, *Gambler's Digest* (Chicago: Follett Publishing Co., 1971), inside front cover.
3. H.R. Lesieur, *The Chase: Career of the Compulsive Gambler* (Garden City, NY: Anchor Books, 1977), p. 73.
4. National Council on Compulsive Gambling, March 1985.
5. Mark Twain, "The Celebrated Jumping Frog," quoted in *The Oxford Dictionary of Quotations* (Oxford, England: Oxford University Press, 1979), p. 554.
6. Robert L. Custer, M.D., "An Overview of Compulsive Gambling" (Unpublished manuscript, 1979).
7. Ernst Simmel, "On Psychoanalysis of the Gambler," *Int. Z. Psychoanal* 6:397 (1924). Quoted in a footnote in Greenberg, "Psychology of Gambling" (Unpublished paper provided the author by the National Council on Compulsive Gambling).
8. *Sharing Recovery Through Gamblers Anonymous* (Los Angeles: Gamblers Anonymous Publishing Co., 1984), pp. 105-8.
9. Telephone conversation between Monsignor Joseph A. Dunne and the author. Quoted with permission.

15

The Gamblers Anonymous Solution

FOR LONGER THAN he cared to admit, Jim W. had directed all his energies toward getting something for nothing. He nearly died from pneumonia when he was only six because he heard about the pot of gold at the foot of the rainbow. His childish mind intrigued by the possibility of instant wealth, he struck out late one rainy afternoon to seek his fortune. A few hours later his parents rushed the frail little boy, soaked to the skin and trembling with cold, to a Los Angeles hospital.

First for Matches, Then for Pennies

In elementary school, Jim and his brothers played cards first for matches, then for pennies, then for higher stakes. By the time he got to high school he was recognized as a formidable poker player. By age 21 he managed a reasonably good living at the card table. Then came the war, and with it a long hitch in the military and expanded opportunities for additional income. Jim capitalized on the many long evenings in the barracks by matching cards with fellow soldiers who seemed to have no urgent need for their regular paychecks.

Jim's return to civilian life coincided with the opening of Santa Anita Racetrack in 1946, and he got a good start in his new civilian profession by winning big in his first wager on the horses. At the same time he made new discoveries in the anesthetic usefulness of booze.

After winning a bundle, Jim celebrated his good fortune by buying drinks for everyone at the lounge nearest the racetrack. After a loss, he consoled himself in a quiet corner with a series of double martinis. When there was no money to bet, he found relief from boredom and depression by lifting a few glasses with the boys at a neighborhood watering hole.

A series of disastrous gambling losses resulted in sorrow-drowning binges that drove Jim to the realization his drinking had become a problem. Frightened, he took his concern to an Alcoholics Anonymous (AA) meeting in Los Angeles and through the 12 steps of AA managed to bring his drinking under control. There he also met Sybil, and soon Jim made her his wife.

Life Is a Gamble and Everyone Does It

A full decade passed, however, before he recognized that his gambling habit was as destructive as his drinking had been. "What is wrong with placing a bet," he had reasoned, "since all of life is a gamble, and everyone gambles one way or another?" But the further he extended this line of reasoning, the more clearly Jim saw certain facts about himself he had preferred to ignore. What was "wrong" with *his* gambling was that it was out of control—and had been, in fact, for years.

He was gambling now only to survive. The more he gambled, the more frenzied became that survival instinct. Life was rapidly losing any identifiable meaning. His desperate wagers produced ruinous financial losses devastating to Sybil. Yet, on the other hand, *not* gambling offered unbearable boredom and restlessness.

In 1954, Jim told his wife he wanted to stop gambling, but that served only to bring a frightened awareness of the strangle hold betting had on him. A conflict arose between the part of him that recognized the destructive nature of his habit and the inner person who had depended for such a long time on the excitement of the games. Looking back years later, Jim described the painful void in his life on the rare occasions when he did manage to refrain from placing bets: "Each day seemed empty. I just had to endure from one hour to the next, because without something to bet on life had little of value to offer."

A Final Fling

Jim's final fling came at the Boulder Club in downtown Las Vegas. He had driven across the desert from Los Angeles, savoring a delicious dream of a future with all his debts paid off, eliminating at last his need to gamble. He had devised what seemed a foolproof system for the crap table. From a new source of credit, he had put together a stake big enough to test and prove his sure-fire scheme. At last he would regain the uncounted thousands of dollars he had lost through the years!

As he walked confidently across the casino floor, Jim listened with relish to the clatter of the slot machines and the familiar chant of the stick men: "Bet the six and

223

eight while you wait . . . double up and catch up . . . bet the lucky field . . . ah, yes, a new lucky shooter coming up!" It was the world he loved, the world in which he belonged and the world which soon would bow at his feet, coveting his skill.

But two hours later Jim felt only the emptiness a gambler knows so well when he senses the end is near. Nothing was working the way it was expected to work. The pit boss was not sweating with anxiety before the threat of Jim's devastating new strategy. He seemed blissfully unaware, in fact, that Jim was even there among all the other losers. The indomitable victor had been reduced to yet another cringing victim of a mercilessly impersonal tyrant—an industry which shrugs off with a Mona Lisa smile all the "systems" that seek to dent its armor, accepting without so much as a "thank you" all offerings laid at its feet.

Down to $1 Bets

Jim had stooped to the ignominity of $1 bets, and his supply of silver dollars was dangerously low. In fact he had exactly 25 of them in his hands and none in his pockets, and as he counted them one more time his thoughts went somehow to Sybil. It had been so long since his patient wife had seen a paycheck that $25 would seem a godsend. But what would a mere $25 solve? Handled the right way, it could prove a respectable stake to launch him on that long-hoped-for winning streak.

By some strange twisting of logic, gambling addicts often feel they would be traitors to other players, if they left the table with money in their hands or pockets. Real gamblers, they have come to believe, never forsake a game until they are totally broke or until they have cleaned out the other participants. "If you can't pay, don't play," the unwritten law of gamblers reminds them.

But transcending all that, on that fateful day at the Boulder Club, Jim shuddered as he thought of the mess he had made of their lives since Sybil placed her confidence in a recovered alcoholic and made him her man.

One Step at a Time

In a rare display of resolution, he dropped the silver dollars in his pockets and turned quickly toward the nearest exit. One step at a time, he moved deliberately away from the tables and the action. He placed one foot in front of the other, shutting out the sights and sounds of the casino floor. The money in his pockets, he kept telling himself, was *theirs,* not *his.* "Small change" though it was, it could be the first installment on a life of freedom from the bondage that held him in its grip for so many wasted years.

Making it safely to the parking lot, he slipped behind the wheel of his car and headed west toward Los Angeles and home.

Time for the Healing Potential

Jim was ready at last. It was time now for the healing potential of that fellowship with others who shared his compulsion. His efforts to stabilize his life and gain strength from other gamblers—in a strategy similar to that of AA—brought him in touch with Tex, Timmy,

Curt, Rocky, Johnny, Red, Art and Bob. Not all of them stuck it out, but the synergism was there. In regular meetings, they talked about their victories and defeats, sharing candidly their hopes and their fears. Valuable publicity came through the Fred Shields talk show on KFI in Los Angeles, and the size of the meetings grew. It was Shields who tagged the group—probably tongue in cheek—as "Gamblers Anonymous."

From that modest beginning, GA has grown to include more than 15,000 self-proclaimed "sick, compulsive gamblers" in nearly 400 American and Canadian groups, plus another 100 groups overseas. With state lotteries proliferating, the number of chapters is increasing rapidly.

For their organization's twenty-fifth anniversary, GA published a limited edition book, *25 Years of Hope, Security, Growth*. In this book, GA states that its program "is a philosophy of living which directs this individual to look within himself for the answers to his dilemma .... It has proven to be the only known hope for those individuals who are caught up in that baffling, insidious addiction known as compulsive gambling.[1]

Only One Thing in Common

Because the organization reaches into all walks of life, participants may find their identification as "sick, compulsive gamblers" the only thing they have in common, but that appears to be all they need. "The individual usually finds himself in a melting pot of doctors, lawyers, cabdrivers and dishwashers," declares the *25 Years*. "He finds a multitude of different religious beliefs and finds there are those who do not believe at all. Yet, in

226

spite of all these differences, he can attempt his recovery, and either by accident or design, assist in the recovery of others."[2]

Gamblers Anonymous is not a Christian ministry. It does urge a dependence upon God, but the concept of God is undefined and unrelated to biblical truth. The four "spiritual steps" in the GA program are described in this way:

1. Came to believe that a power greater than ourselves can restore us to a normal way of thinking and living.

2. Made a decision to turn our wills and our lives over to the care of this power of our own understanding.

3. Humbly ask God (of our understanding) to remove our shortcomings.

4. Sought through prayer and meditation to improve our conscious contact with God as we understand him, praying only for knowledge of his will for us and the power to carry that out.[3]

Six Basic Truths

Gamblers Anonymous does not impose a regimented philosophy upon its participants, but it does require complete acceptance of six basic truths concerning the nature of gambling addiction:

227

1. Gambling is a progressive illness.

2. It always gets worse, but never better.

3. It can only be arrested and may never be cured, regardless of the time of abstinence.

4. It can only be arrested through total abstinence.

5. It is a baffling, insidious, compulsive addiction.

6. In its worst form, it can very easily lead to demoralization, insanity and death.

In the first of three steps of admittance, the candidate must confess what previously may have been obvious to everyone but himself: that his life has become unmanageable. Mounting indebtedness, serious marital problems and tensions at work usually make that conclusion not difficult to come by.

A Disease Difficult to Diagnose

Diagnosing a gambling psychosis, like diagnosing alcoholism, is seldom an exact science. The power of gambling over an individual's life has many shades and degrees, and not every victim fits a specific profile. What at first may have been a purely recreational indulgence may suddenly be seen as an illness in need of therapy. Fortunately, formulas have been devised by which that fact usually can be determined. That diagnosis of dependency, however, may not lead to a solution unless the victim himself or herself accepts without reservation the humbling classification of "addict." Through the combined experiences of its participants, GA has developed a list of 20 questions that probe deeply into the minds of those who find themselves wondering. Should you, by chance, be wondering, you might try them on for size:

1. Did you ever lose time from work due to gambling?

2. Has gambling ever made your home life unhappy?

3. Did gambling affect your reputation?

4. Have you ever felt remorse after gambling?

5. Did you ever gamble to get money with which to pay debts or otherwise solve financial difficulties?

6. Did gambling cause a decrease in your ambition or efficiency?

7. After losing, did you feel you must return as soon as possible and win back your losses?

8. After a win, did you have a strong urge to return and win more?

9. Did you often gamble until your last dollar was gone?

10. Did you ever borrow to finance your gambling?

11. Have you ever sold anything to finance gambling?

12. Were you reluctant to use "gambling money" for normal expenditures?

13. Did gambling make you careless of the welfare of your family?

14. Did you ever gamble longer than you had planned?

15. Have you ever gambled to escape worry or trouble?

16. Have you ever committed, or considered committing, an illegal act to finance gambling?

17. Did gambling cause you to have difficulty in sleeping?

18. Do arguments, disappointments or frustrations create within you an urge to gamble?

19. Did you ever have an urge to celebrate good fortune by a few hours of gambling?

20. Have you ever considered self-destruction as a result of your gambling?[4]

A yes answer to as few as seven of these 20 questions might serve as a warning that experienced counseling now could save you untold agony in years to come.

A World of Plenty and Largesse

The GA program addresses a dream world common to all compulsive gamblers—a world composed of all the great and wonderful things they are going to do when they make that big win. Gamblers generally see themselves as philanthropic and quite charming people. They picture themselves as inhabiting a world of plenty and largesse, made possible by the huge sums of money to be handed them when their "system" begins to work or when their luck changes. Luxuries that challenge the imagination lie just beyond their reach— luxuries to be shared gladly and generously with those long-neglected loved ones and friends who deserve much better treatment than they have received.

Ironically, even winning does not make those dreams come true. When compulsive gamblers do win, they almost invariably gamble again to weave even grander dreams—obsessed by the idea that Lady Luck finally is smiling and that the time for the big kill has come. If they lose again, they gamble on in reckless determination to get it all back, and more.

As Mickey Rooney has allegedly described his own half-century of betting: "When I was just a kid, I lost two dollars in a crap game, and I've lost over a million dollars since then trying to get those two dollars back!"

Unfathomable to the Nongambler

The depth of the compulsive gambler's misery is unfathomable to the nongambler because it lies in territory uncharted by the rational mind. Again and again, the addict's dream world comes crashing down, making his innocent loved ones unwilling victims of his folly. After each reversal, he struggles back, dreams more dreams and loses yet another time. Many compulsive gamblers could testify to their identification with the First Murderer in *Macbeth*, who mourns:

> So weary with disasters, tugg'd with fortune;
> That I would set my life on any chance,
> To mend it or be rid on't.[5]

The compulsive gambler must continue to dream, and he must continue to believe his dreams soon will come true. No amount of logic can convince him that his grand schemes will not someday transport him into the realm of lasting prosperity—place him for all the world to see and admire in a permanent winner's circle. All trust seems wrapped in that overpowering expectation. Without that dream and without that hope, life as he has come to define it simply would not be worth the struggle or the suspense. And so, unless something, somewhere, somehow stops him in his tracks and brings him back to reality, the compulsive gambler goes on through life pursuing his unfulfilled dreams and those never-ending rainbows in his ceaseless quest for that nonexistent pot of gold.

232

1. If you were a parent to Jim W. when he was a school-boy, in what way might you have intervened in his life and prevented the gambling addiction that proved so devastating in later years? Do you feel his childish search for the pot of gold at the foot of the rainbow indicated he was predisposed to a lifelong search for "something for nothing"? How might a wise and spiritually discerning parent have channeled that tendency into something constructive?

2. To quote Jim's question, "What *is* wrong with placing a bet, since all of life is a gamble and everyone gambles one way or another?" Thoughtful Christians have asked why buying life insurance or stock shares shouldn't be classified also as gambling. Do you see a difference between those activities and betting on a horse or playing poker for a quarter?

3. In view of Jim's lack of willpower for so many years, what do you think happened that enabled him to walk away from that casino, take his money home to his wife and eventually found Gambler's Anonymous? Though nothing is said in GA about Christian commitment, do you feel God was involved in Jim's sudden and miraculous recovery? If so, can you support that idea with a Bible verse?

4. Do the four "spiritual steps" of Gambler's Anonymous resemble in any way the commitment we believe necessary for a person to receive Christ as Saviour? What about the six basic truths each GA member must acknowledge? Do these, plus the con-

fession that life has become unmanageable, suggest a "religious" aspect to the GA program?

5. If you "like to do a little gambling yourself now and then," have you checked yourself out with the 20 questions Gamblers Anonymous has developed to help people face up to the reality of their own addiction? Remember that yes to as few as seven of those questions suggests the possibility of a problem of compulsion!

Notes

1. Gamblers Anonymous, *25 Years of Hope, Security, Growth* (Los Angeles: Gamblers Anonymous Publishing Inc., 1982).
2. Ibid.
3. Gamblers Anonymous, *Combined Pamphlet* (Los Angeles: Gamblers Anonymous Publishing Inc.).
4. Ibid., pp. 15-16. According to GA's National Executive Secretary, members refer to this small publication as the "combo book" and state that it is "like a bible to us."
5. William Shakespeare, *Macbeth*, i, 112. Quoted in *Bartlett's Familiar Quotations* (Boston: Little, Brown & Company, 1980), p. 238.

16
The Case in a Nutshell

ALLOW ME TO STATE, then, in the fewest possible words and the simplest possible terms why gambling, from the biblically literate Christian's point of view, is "weighed in the balances and art found wanting" (Dan. 5:27).

First Is Stewardship Responsibility

Let me phrase it in two different realms of logic, touching *first* upon the matter of stewardship responsibility:

Everything we have, in reality, belongs to the Lord—and how often we recite that truth with appropriate humility. Whether we buy with it, burn it, bury it or bet with it, our money is not our own.

Does the Christian who frequents casinos, racetracks and back-room poker games take a moment, before each wager to seek divine guidance as to which number, card, horse or dog he and the Lord should bet on? That is not likely. But if he did, his prayer would go something like this: "Heavenly Father, you and I brought along only $50 of our money, so please do something about how the cards or the dice turn up or which horse runs fastest. And don't forget, Lord, you get one-tenth if we win."

Our heathen predecessors, obsessed with ideas of the gods, demons and other unseen forces that controlled their environment, and ignorant of the God who at last has revealed Himself, reasoned along those lines. I have a feeling the Lord's response to the gambler's prayer would be "Where do you get that 'we' stuff? *It's all mine anyway,* to give or to take, to be generous or spare, to use or to destroy. Whatever gave you the superstitious notion I am yours to exploit—like some pagan good luck charm—or that I've reason to make you prosper at the gambling table?"

One Need Met Makes a Difference

When the $50 is gone, will the errant believer give any thought to the hungry mouths that money might have fed, the destitute it might have clothed or what it would have meant to some faithful missionary trying to raise travel expenses back to his field of labor? "Come on!" he pleads in self-defense. "I give to the church already. I don't have any way of knowing who the needy people are, and I couldn't help all of them if I did!" The fact is, we wouldn't have to search very far or very long to find at least *one* person in need. In this world of tragic physical and spiritual malnutrition, one need met is enough to make a crucial difference.

Yes, gambling distorts our concept and clouds our view of Christian stewardship.

Gambling Violates the First Commandment

In our *second* realm of logic, gambling is a subtle but culpable violation of the first commandment: "Thou shalt have no other gods before me." What, after all, are Lady Luck and Dame Fortune but substitute figures for God?

That statement, I am well aware, will generate reaction covering a full spectrum of human emotions—all the way from hostility and ridicule at one end to possible enthusiastic accord at the other. Never mind—we can be comfortable with either. We should be neither surprised, disturbed nor offended when believing people disagree. There are well-meaning if undiscerning Christians who consider gambling a harmless recreational diversion and see no moral or spiritual reason to deny themselves or others that pleasure—"as long as we can afford it." From the perspective of the Body of Christ, that point of view is tragically shortsighted.

Every Dollar Has a Significant Potential

For reasons best known to Himself, God remains sovereignly aloof from any dependence upon our coin of the realm. As far as our heavenly Father's personal needs are concerned, it is as if money and other forms of material wealth did not exist. In His wisdom, however, He has made money a primary medium for and proof of human trust and obedience. Because of the ambivalence and fleeting values it creates, money can become the basis for the most crucial tests of our faith. All too often, we fail the test by declaring the money to be our god.

237

From the practical point of view, human suffering cannot be assuaged and the world cannot be evangelized without money to provide the materials, to support the work and the workers. Wherever we look, the needs are overwhelming. Yet many believers are involved financially only as a token of their intellectual assent to the authority and integrity of Christ. Every dollar that does become available, therefore, has a significant potential in the worldwide ministry of the gospel. Never in the history of the Church has Christ's work on earth been adequately financed.

Gambling Clouds the Issue of "God"

I am grateful for some believers who do share my concerns, but I have encountered also either cordial amusement or undisguised hostility—at times both—from my suggestion that gambling diverts the Christian's attention from our Creator/Redeemer/Sustainer and makes some other "god" the imagined source of our sustenance. That line of reasoning seems to me so logical that the question in need of an answer is not "Is it true?" but the more cynical "Does it really matter?"

It matters very much. Truth is truth, whether or not it has the support of human reasoning or majority opinion, and whether or not it is understood by its detractors. "But the natural man receiveth not the things of the Spirit of God: for they are foolishness unto him: neither can he know them, because they are spiritually discerned" (1 Cor. 2:14).

The doctrine we deal with here is elusive precisely because it lies in a uniquely shrouded area of spiritual perception. It has a challenging and painful personal application. It stresses the eternal but unwelcome truth that those of us who belong to Christ are people who lay rightful claim to nothing because we were purchased off the slave market of sin. We are not our own. The deed and title to our lives rests in the hands of the One who purchased us with His own vicarious death (see 1 Cor. 6:19).

The Love of Money: Still the Root of Evil

As a means of exchanging wealth, gambling reverses the biblical value system. It is a strategy for financial gain in defiance of Paul's solemn warning to Timothy: "For the love of money is the root of all evil: which while some coveted after, they have erred from the faith, and pierced themselves through with many sorrows" (1 Tim. 6:10).

"Love" of money implies *worship* of money and *trust* in money. The love of money stands as a fierce competitor to the love of God. The believer who clings to his right to "a little recreational gambling" may consider the apostle's words unpalatable or, more ominous yet, irrelevant—but he will also find them tragically prophetic. Paul's epistles to Timothy are part of the reliable and authoritative Word of God. We cannot, after all, love God and *mammon*—the Aramaic word for "riches" or "personal wealth."

The Irony, Inconsistency and Irrationality

That love of money inevitably will place the gambling Christian with strange and spiritually draining bedfellows. The "sleaze factor" is ever present in gaming circles and, in chapter after chapter of this book, we have introduced you to real people and real occurrences, colorfully and convincingly illustrating the irony, inconsistency and irrationality of gambling. It would be difficult to imagine a faithful witness to the saving power of Jesus Christ attempting to share his or her faith over a craps table, roulette wheel or poker pot—or at a bingo party, for that matter.

It is urgent that we Christians learn to be content with what we have and leave the matter of our personal prosperity in the good hands of God.

Gambling, not just incidentally, compromises the divine pronouncement that those who will not work may not eat (see 2 Thess. 3:10)—a stern but realistic biblical principle upon which our all-but-forgotten Judeo-Christian work ethic is based.

Imagine Jesus Betting on the Dallas Cowboys

For the courageous few willing to stretch their minds on this point, it would be interesting to imagine Jesus trying His luck at blackjack, betting on the Dallas Cowboys with His bookie, screaming for a lucky seven at the craps table—or even methodically placing His little round chips on the numbers at a church bingo party.

The Christian's Responsibility for Others

Finally, but certainly not least in terms of significance, the Christian who defends his indulgence in wagering must also consider his responsibility in the spread of the endemic disease called "compulsive gambling." Let me show you why through the case of Kathy K. (not her real name).

We mention Kathy's case here because she represents a broadening segment of churchgoing Americans on the cutting edge of a lingering controversy. They have helped change what once was perceived as a harmless family activity into an issue Catholic leaders now acknowledge they must "seriously rethink." The issue? Church-sponsored bingo games.

In fact, in Houma, Louisiana, Bishop Warren L. Boudreaux already has ordered parishes in his diocese to phase out their weekly bingo nights and other fundraisers that involve gambling. Using gambling to raise church funds is "unworthy of our God," he told parish priests in a letter forbidding certain games of chance after the end of the year. By mid-1991, even bingo and raffles will be banned entirely in his diocese.

"I am convinced that we will never teach our people the stewardship of money as long as any of these means are used for the purposes of church support," the bishop wrote in his letter announcing the ban. His parishioners are not likely to celebrate the new policy, but in the Catholic hierarchy they have little choice but to comply.[1]

Now back to Kathy K., whose experience seems to confirm the bishop's statement.

"A Little Personal Problem"

When Kathy K. called me for help in a counseling session "with a little personal problem," she was hesitant and apologetic because "It's kind of embarrassing

241

to admit I've gotten myself into such a stupid situation."
She was two months behind in her mortgage payments
when she came to me for counsel, and the savings-and-
loan people were beginning to apply pressure. She knew
her husband would take care of the problem if she told
him about it, but she couldn't do that because she didn't
want him to know how irrationally she had acted. The
fact is, he gave her cash to pay the mortgage each
month, but she had lost the money gambling.

At a gaming table perhaps? She lived in Las Vegas or
Atlantic City—right? Or was she over her head at the
games in the back room of her country club? Or maybe
it was her bookie, her bridge club or an illegal gambling
den where patrons are admitted only after recognition
through one of those little peep-holes in the door?

None of the above. Kathy K. lost it all in church. In
church? Yes, she was a church bingo addict, a compulsive gambler. She had been losing consistently for six
months or more, and the more she lost the more recklessly she bet. She had managed to take care of the
mortgage payments for part of that time by juggling
other accounts and borrowing money from her mother.
But now she was completely over her head, and all
because of those "harmless" and altogether legal
church bingo parties.

A Purely Recreational Activity—at First

Kathy K.'s fate might have seemed unlikely when the
Catholic Church first inaugurated its bingo games. "It
was begun years ago as a purely recreational activity in a
few of our larger parishes," says Bishop Norbert Dorsey
of the South Florida Diocese. "It seemed innocent

enough in the beginning, and the cost of participation was no more than a night at the movies or many other forms of entertainment. The prospect of winning made it exciting for our people, and the losses as well as the rewards are modest."

I asked him how important parish bingo parties are to his Church as fund-raising strategies.

"Bingo never has been a significant source of income, but it certainly has helped in the upkeep of the fabric of the Church," Bishop Dorsey responded. "There's always the burden of the Catholic school system, and there are other costs that often go a bit beyond income from contributions.

"Our people—particularly some of the older ones—always responded well to bingo, probably because the excitement of taking a chance on something is part of our nature. Bingo is a simple game that is easily learned, and it proved a good 'family night' activity that helped bring our people together in social situations." Though Catholic clergymen do not stress the fact, bingo also involves a substantial number of non-Catholics in the financial support of that Church.

"Excess" Rears Its Ugly Head

Bishop Dorsey acknowledges, however, that bingo now has gone beyond a simple family affair in too many cases. The ugly word, "excess," has reared its unlovely head. In larger metropolitan areas, Catholics and non-Catholics alike go from parish to parish several nights of the week, motivated primarily by gambling fever and the greed that is its unvarying symptom. "People have misused the activity, and for some, yes, bingo has become just another form of gambling," Bishop Dorsey says.[2]

That creates problems of consistency for their Church because many of its clergy are alarmed by the emerging of more serious forms of gambling as a "national pastime" in America and have taken a stand against it. Catholic leaders generally align themselves for ethical as well as religious reasons with anticasino, antilottery and other movements to restrict gambling.

This dichotomy has confused the average parishioner. He has experienced difficulty in accepting the strange reasoning that makes a church bingo parlor perfectly licit, socially correct and religiously acceptable while, at the same time, a casino or bolita running is illegal, unethical or sinful. It is far from clear by what criteria one form of gambling—enjoying the sanctuary of a church—can be declared legal while another—separate from any church building—is a violation of the law.

Meanwhile, with increasing frequency, pastoral counselors witness the devastation of compulsive gambling on people like Kathy K. The trend now is toward dealing with that troublesome inconsistency.

Can "the Church" Provide an Alternative?

"The Church now is calling upon all its people to rethink the role and the purpose of bingo as a recreational and fund-raising activity," Bishop Dorsey says. One difficulty Louisiana's Bishop Boudreaux may face is that no one is sure the church can provide an alternative in the area of recreation and excitement. "Stopping our bingo games is going to mean depriving some of our older people—and even younger families—of a harmless recreational activity," Bishop Dorsey explains. "We must find something that will take the place of that in their lives."[3]

Respectfully and in all sincerity, I have some suggestions. They spring from the promise of Romans 8:32: "He that spared not his own Son, but delivered him up for us all, how shall he not with him also freely give us all things?" "All things" surely include the ability to program those tedious hours. We can fill them with excitement and challenges unique to those whose lives yield to the claims and depend upon the promises of Jesus Christ.

We can increase biblical literacy, broaden our knowledge of God and the needs of His world, resolve our debilitating problems of human relationships, encourage individual steps of faith, nurture personal spiritual growth and involve believers in evangelism, missions and the building of the Kingdom of God. If those suggestions seem invalid to some bingo devotees, then perhaps they would find themselves lonely and bored in heaven itself, should they arrive there one day.

I Rest My Case

On that note, I am happy to rest my case. For the Christian, the discipline of choices never ceases. Paul's prayer for His young Macedonian converts—and the Holy Spirit's prayer for us—is that we might possess "a love that is full of knowledge and every wise insight . . . to be able always to recognize the highest and the best, and to live sincere and blameless lives until the day of Christ" (Phil. 1:9-10, *Phillips*). That admonition reminds us that the choice for a Christian seldom is merely between right and wrong. The subtle challenge in decision making for the believer lies in choosing between what seems all right on the one hand and what is better on the other.

No doubt you aspire to the delights and the fruit of that spiritual plateau Paul described—recognizing "the highest and the best." If you think you can do it with one foot in the Promised Land and the other knee bowed in supplication to the Goddess of Chance, I would offer one final word of admittedly unsolicited advice:

Don't bet on it, dear brother or sister—just *don't bet on it!*

Points to Ponder

1. Do you feel a Christian's stewardship responsibility extends to the "extra" money he might use to make a wager? In view of the spiritual and material needs of the world, is there really any such thing as money we can "spare"? What Bible verse would you quote to prove everything we have belongs, in reality, to God?

2. What does the author mean when he refers to "spiritual malnutrition"? Is that a condition that afflicts only the unchurched in our world? Is it possible for people who hold proper Bible-believing credentials and speak the evangelical language convincingly to be spiritually undernourished as well? On a scale that progresses upwards from 1 to 10, how would you classify your own spiritual diet?

3. What is your response to the suggestion that gambling clouds the issue of God—who He is, what He

wants from us, what He does for us and what He has in mind for us? Would you support or reject the suggestion that gambling diverts attention from our Creator/Redeemer/Sustainer and makes some other "god" the source of our sustenance?

4. In 1 Timothy 6:10, the "root of all evil" is identified as "the love of money." In what way have you personally found that statement to be prophetic? Obviously, the Christian must live like everyone else as a participant in our monetary system. But is it possible for a believer—even a rich believer—to have a different attitude toward money than unbelievers?

5. The author refers to "the irony, inconsistency and irrationality" of gambling. Do you know of a gambling activity where those descriptive words would not apply? Do you feel you could be an effective witness to Christ's redeeming work in your life if you were part of the crowd around a craps table or a roulette wheel?

Notes
1. *Miami Herald,* September 25, 1986, sect. 1, p. 5.
2. Bishop Norbert Dorsey, Diocese of South Florida, in personal interview with author, September 13, 1986. Quoted with permission.
3. Ibid.

Bibliography

Allan, D. D. *The Nature of Gambling.* New York: Coward-McCann, 1952.

Bergler, Edmund. *The Psychology of Gambling.* London: International Universities Press, 1974.

Chafetz, H. *Play the Devil: A History of Gambling in the United States.* New York: Clarkson N. Potter, Inc., 1960.

Herman, Robert D. *Gamblers and Gambling.* Lexington, MA: Lexington Books, 1976.

Hoffman, William, Jr. *The Loser.* New York: Funk & Wagnalls Inc., 1968.

LeSieur, H. R. *The Chase—Career of the Compulsive Gambler.* Garden City, NY: Anchor Books, 1977.

Moody, Gordon E. *Social Control of Gambling.* London: The Churches' Council on Gambling, 1974.

Newman, Otto. *Gambling: Hazard and Reward.* London: Althone Press, 1972.

Scott, Marvin. *The Racing Game.* Chicago: Aldine Publishing Co., 1968.

Starkey, L. M. *Money, Mania and Morals: The Churches and Gambling.* New York: Abingdon Press, 1964.